The Enemy's Tactical Manual and A Christian Call to Arms

By Randal S. Kinkade

Copyright 2011 by Randal S. Kinkade

The Enemy's Tactical Manual
and a Christian Call to Arms
By Randal S. Kinkade

All rights reserved solely by the author. The author guarantees all contents are original and do not infringe upon the legal rights of any other person or work. No part of this book may be reproduced in any form without the permission of the author. The views expressed in this book are not necessarily those of the publisher.

ISBN 978-1-7376594-0-2

Unless otherwise indicated Bible quotations are taken from the New King James Version of the Bible.
Copyright 1982 by Thomas Nelson, Inc.

Published by Willow River Publishing

To Sam and Max.
For asking questions
and seriously pondering the answers.

Table of Contents

Preface	5
PART ONE	
The Enemy's Tactical Manual	
Introductory Letter from the Cunning Dragon	10
Know the Enemy	15
Observation and Target Selection	27
Tools and Devices of an Effective Warrior	49
Applying the Tactics	71
PART TWO	
A Christian Call to Arms	
Understanding Our Enemy	76
Preparation	80
Prayer	87
Our Strength and Our Weaknesses	96
Assuring Our Spot on the Continuum	100
Intellectual Defense	114
Our Calling	122
Overcoming the Devices of the Enemy	129
The Battle, The Love and The Reward	146

PREFACE

When I worked in law enforcement, I would often think of what the bad guys were up to based on what I knew of criminal behavior. I asked myself what I would do in their circumstance in order to do my job more effectively. This is how I approach the idea of spiritual warfare in this book.

The Bible explicitly tells us that we have opposition to our relationship with God. As a church, if we approach the subject at all we typically do it in a cursory fashion. Most will agree that there is an enemy but don't know how to effectively engage him. To know that we have an enemy is not enough. To be successful in overcoming him, we need to understand his goals, and how he plans to execute them.

In "The Art of War" Sun Tzu writes: "You must accomplish your attack and escape unharmed. This requires foreknowledge." This is an opportunity for you to see into the thoughts of your adversary and discover how he works against you. Having this foreknowledge gives you the tools needed to defend, and to move forward, the Kingdom of God.

The intent of this book is to show you the guile of the enemy from his perspective.

Here you will find the tactics of your enemy and the promise of your God. Under-standing both will guarantee success.

John 10:10 tells us *"The thief does not come except to steal, kill and destroy"*. It is the desire of our enemy to distort this truth in any way he can to cause you to stumble and ultimately fall. Looking at the intent of our enemy and then developing our defense from a biblical perspective will help to overcome these distortions.

The bible instructs us that this battle is ongoing and that we can't overcome our enemy alone. Take what you read here seriously because your adversary would love for you to be unaware. Don't rush in without proper study and back up but don't stand and watch without offering yourself up either. You are protected by the work of Jesus upon the cross and His authority granted to you. (See Matt 11:12, Luke 9:1-2 and Mark 13:34)

If you are already engaged in this battle the information provided here will help you to be a better warrior. If you attend church and read the bible, and are thinking, "Come on. Do I really need to worry about demons?" reading further will give you information as to how and why you may have those thoughts. Notice the intellectual battle happening in your head. That is one possible manifestation of this spiritual battle. As you read on, don't be surprised if see yourself described at times in these pages.

I confess that I have an admiration for Satan. Not in who he is but in how he works as an opponent in this battle. I don't care to get too close, but I see how he uses me against myself and I recognize his superior ability. We know from the Bible that his objective is to keep us from the kingdom of heaven and to separate us from God. The only way we can win this battle is to engage the tools God has provided and to call on Jesus to lead us.

You and I don't deal with Satan directly. He has a more ambitious goal. We deal with his minion. They, however, have the same objective in mind. We also struggle with products of a fallen world and of our own fleshly lusts. Not every bad day is caused by a dark angel. For the purposes of this book, however, you should rely on the premise that anything that is adverse to you spiritually is a part of your spiritual battle. The general defense is the same no matter where the attack begins. Rely on the work of Christ in your life whether the attack is from the flesh, the world or the enemy.

This enemy is real and can be a hazard but your main focus should not be on them. Keep your focus on Jesus. If you obsess over these dark angels and your obsession keeps you away from engaging in the spiritual battle out of fear, the demons win. If, while engaged in spiritual interaction, you see a demon around every corner and in every mishap or situation, and this obsession causes you to miss the beauty of

God in the situations of your life, the demons win again. But if you know demons exist, understand how they work against the kingdom of God and set off to work for God's kingdom with your focus on Him, you are assured victory.

PART ONE

The Enemy's Tactical Manual

INTRODUCTORY LETTER FROM THE CUNNING DRAGON A SERVANT OF LUCIFER OUR HIGH KING

Warriors of Deception in the service of The Cunning Dragon, I have devised this handbook to advance the success of my battalion in the mission our High King has set before us. (May he rule forever.)

The following pages contain the techniques and tactics you are to employ to achieve victory over the despicable servants of The Ancient of Days and ultimately over The Ancient One himself!

Understand that not all generals of our High King, such as I, will agree with certain philosophies and tactics offered in these pages. Because of this I demand that this tome stay within our battalion only. We are an elite group and many of your compatriots (so called) are using elementary tactics that are ineffective on the advanced targets I wish to destroy. I will discuss those tactics with brevity so you know of them, as they are useful for the elementary work of weaker targets, but we are going after a much richer achievement. A target that, when won, causes The

Ancient One extreme heartbreak and sorrow. **That is our goal!**

You all will remember our proper decision to leave the presence of The Ancient One for the rich life of sharing in the rule of this earthly kingdom. Our king is lord of this world and we are willing and active participants in his goal to do irreparable harm to The Ancient One's "children".

What he sees in them I do not understand and, in fact, I need not understand his desire for them. None of us do. All we need to know is the more we keep from him, or better, turn from him, the more we gain the respect of our lord and High King.

You may have heard of the rule of not putting our battle plans in a permanent, tangible form but there are times when even those whom I serve miss the obvious points of communication and combat. So, as I know you are loyal to me, I trust you will never pass these techniques on to other battle groups. Let them fend for themselves. Besides, we are the elite; there is no sense in bringing others to our level and then having to share the glory of our victories. Let the lesser generals lead their own teams with their own tired tactics.

Of course, you will occasionally have the unpleasant duty of taking on physical form. When that is your assignment commit this volume to memory. Never take it into the realm of our human enemy!

Knowledge is power. Do not be guilty of granting these vermin any power.

Our best and most wonderful tactic is one of misdirection. If our regular techniques become known their effectiveness will be compromised. You do not want to be a party to that faux pas. You best neither test nor toy with my wrath.

Before you begin understand two things from my perspective as your general:

1) I admire our supreme commander's knowledge and ability to do as he has promised- to make us rulers of the world of The Ancient One's vermin.
2) And I have done enough study into what The Ancient One has promised to his people to believe that, contrary to what our High King proclaims, our end could very well be upon us.

The Forbidden Book, the last of their so-called "Holy Scripture", leads me to believe the possibility of this end. Never mind how I know what this Forbidden Book contains, suffice it to say that as an honored leader of our High King's loyal troops I have been granted certain privileges in this regard. Having looked ahead I interpret the document differently than we were once led to believe.

Our High King tells us that because so much detail is given in these "scriptures" about the past that those passages are written from a point of knowledge, but in the forbidden book the passages about the final outcome are short and vague, therefore speculative. The High King interprets this as meaning there is no ultimate defeat of his kingdom and we yet have the upper hand. He contends no foreknowledge is truly in place about the outcome of the final battle.

I look at it differently. Consider this: If I am wrong, and I would gladly concede to this after the final battles, the tactics in this tome will ensure a bevy of human slaves for us to play with and to do our bidding forever.

But if I am right, and when have you known me not to be, our main objective must be to harm The Ancient One in the deepest manner possible with the time we have afforded to us. These creatures have free will and it is The Ancient One's desire that they choose him over everything else. Our assignment then is quite easy; convince, coerce, frighten, entice or intimidate them to choose *anything* else.

The pain caused in the heart of the one who rejected us and sent us here is my satisfaction. I want more of that satisfaction. I want The Ancient One to look upon our captives for eternity and feel the pain of their rejection. You, my dear soldiers, are the machinations of my satisfaction—and his pain.

To this end study and employ these tools to wreak all disruption in the blossoming relationship between The Ancient One and his so called "beloved" (Oh if I

were in human form that term would make me wretch!)
Forever your General,
                The Cunning Dragon

KNOW THE ENEMY

Our enemy, of course, is The Ancient of Days. That is well known. However, since the time we chose to follow our king to this planet, we no longer can approach The Ancient One and thus we cannot attack Him directly. We do, however, have the ability to damage his heart! Anything that we can do to cause that effect is our mission.

The Ancient One adores those weak, secondary creatures he created to frolic on this world of our King. So our aim is to destroy the objects of his affection. Forget a direct assault on The Ancient One. Our King has that access and has chosen not to use it for battle. Many who have served with me started out with a giddiness that this sort of confrontation was possible in the heavenlies. Do not think it so! If the writings are correct in this matter we will have the opportunity to battle here, on our territory, soon enough. Until then we should endeavor to move ahead that time line by the spiritual destruction of these vermin who populate our physical world.

So, our objective, and thus the focus of my plan, is these weak creatures that The Ancient One loves. Everyone we push, entice or lead off his path pierces his heart and causes him great sorrow. His rulebook states that he wants none to perish, but they must follow his rules. Our mission is to lead our prey to misunderstand their responsibility to those rules, or to believe they have a just cause to break them.

A poor warrior allows the justified sense of pride to overtake them in their mission hoping for immediate recognition. You, my best warriors, must leave your rightful sense of pride behind for the short term and encourage these vermin to grow in their false pride and self worth in order to lead them into our waiting grip. Then, and only then, can we sit back and sip the nectar of our victory as we watch their torment and revel in the sorrow of The Ancient One.

To that purpose I will instruct you of their strengths (few) and how to exploit them. A crafty assailant patiently plucks away at their strengths. The weaknesses almost take care of themselves yet we should still touch on them.

There really are too many for me to cover here so I will be brief for two reasons.

> 1) When you worked for other generals you no doubt used these weaknesses against your target. You should already be familiar. (Consider all of their animal instincts such as hunger, sexual drive, the need for love and comfort etc. and you will have a generous list to choose from.)
> 2) We will use these only to set up a base of operation within a strong enemy.

Our mission is to exploit their strengths and bring our target toppling into our hands. So as a reminder: these creatures are nothing more than glorified animals with the same basic needs and drives as any piece of flesh. We can always use these drives against them. And we will, but simply to erode away their resolve so that their strengths will crumble. Since the time that the first man willingly gave this world to Our High King there have been characteristics inherent in man that we can, and should, exploit. Some may be too obvious for those who are spiritually mature; like adultery or fornication or lewdness. But it is a simple thing to wear your target down and to use even these things to their undoing.

There are others though that we can and will use regularly. Some of my favorites are: covetousness, deceit, pride (oh, the simplicity of pride) and foolishness. These are things that you should use whenever you have the opportunity. They not only weaken your target but they spread like a well-placed virus to others around them.

Our true targets are the ones who have a strong desire to explore, or who have already developed a relationship with The Ancient One. This relationship, fully understood and developed, is their only real strength.

Because our targets are at the stage where they know The Ancient One we must weaken their resolve and stop their progress. The best way to exploit their animal nature is with subtlety. Never make your advances obvious. It shows your weakness as a warrior if you fall into this trap. Our King has invested centuries leading a majority of humankind into believing we do not exist. We must do our work in such a way as to continue that belief.

Weak warriors want to destroy their target but they want even more the recognition of doing so. Our kingdom loses more opportunities to this fault than to any other. This battalion is needed because of the failings of our lesser contemporaries who refuse to use their self-control. Do not fall back into that state. If the target already has knowledge of The Ancient One it is easy for an ally to point out our presence. We must camouflage that presence. If you hear your target talking to a fellow follower about the troubles he is having and the fellow follower says something like, "Do you think this could be spiritual warfare?" You have been too obvious. Your camouflage is failing.

The successful warrior uses the target against himself with subtle whispers. Watch your subject and become intimate with his personality; know his personal animal weaknesses and explore the areas where he has already made covenants with us, or himself, that you can use as an entry point. Beware of the areas where he is strong. Do not go to that battlefield directly. You can wear away at it indirectly until it falters then start to plant doubt and opposing covenants to bring down that strength.

For example, let us say your target has a strong defense against sexual lust. He is an upstanding member of his church and is well respected by his peers. Help him to feel good about being well loved and continually whisper of how good he is to garner such love. Open the door to pride. Now bring in a woman who is struggling with a question of faith caused by a failing relationship with man who is not a follower of The Ancient One. Be sure your target sees her distraught and silently crying for help. Remind him that he is a good man, and he is the one who can help this poor soul. His pride, if sown well, will take hold of part of this relationship and as you allow him to minister to this woman, she will feel the love she was missing with her man. She will be restored in her faith and owe it all to him. (I know some of you are concerned at her renewal of faith. After all, are we not trying to bring her down as well? Remember our goal is to bring down the strong so many follow.)

Now that she feels saved by her new hero, she will faun over him. Keep whispering to his pride and he will puff up every time he sees her. Lead him to wonder where she is when she misses a meeting and have him comment on noticing her absence when she returns. Her happiness at his acknowledgement will steer her to move even closer to him and his pride will allow her to do so. He will say to himself "There is nothing sexual here. I just have a new sister in the faith. Let him believe that until he finally falls.

It starts with the deeper, longer look; the realization that not only does she admire his strength but that she is attractive physically as well. Then her light touch to his arm and later his taking her hand as she enters the sanctuary. Next it is a hug then it is a meeting after their services at the coffee shop.

You see the trap is deliberately slow. You must be patient. Never push too hard. You want him to fall but you have time. His status, being well respected in the church, is a key element of this attack. When he falls into her arms at the end of your campaign all those who see it or hear of it through others will have a panel torn from their armor as well.

You have now opened doors for our troops to work in all who admired him. He falls, he uses her as his medication during his humiliation, he takes it out on her and she knows not why, and she leaves in anger, confusion and frustration never to return to the church. (See how your earlier fears of bringing her further in to the kingdom of The Ancient One have been overcome?)

The fissures in their strength are your way in. Nearly all of the characteristics you would count as strengths have an edge that you can get your fingernail underneath. Take your time and whisper into those weak areas so that your voice becomes their voice. Work on getting the target to agree with your voice.

When he trips whisper to him "You are such an idiot; what a fool; who can take you seriously", and the like. Deliver these things slowly but with sharp focus. The victory begins when you hear the target mutter, "I am such an idiot. No one will ever take me seriously" Now you have him! This, my dear warrior, is a covenant. You have whispered, he has agreed and taken ownership of the statement. It is now he who degrades himself. Once a covenant is made it requires only minor maintenance to keep alive and it is an open door for you to enter, with full permission of the subject.

Though we will rarely have the simplicity of working on those who do not feel the need to reach for The Ancient One, (Our targets are the ones lost by less astute warriors to this deplorable state) probe the actions and the words of your target for clues to past covenants. Many are carried over into their new relationship with The Ancient One. It is very common, for instance, that a target will accept that he is forgiven by The Ancient One but has no ability to forgive himself. This is a rich opening. As long as your target has these feelings of self doubt, or better yet, self-loathing, no matter who put it there, you can capitalize on it for our gain.

Let me offer an example of how I used my cunning against a target's defenses.

He was a lover of the wilderness and had been taught of The Ancient One in a church that we kept ineffective through incomplete teachings. The son of The Ancient One was courting him in the wilderness so I stepped in.

He was unaware of the access he provided me so I talked with him when he was out in the woods. I cooed love songs into his heart feigning The Ancient One's voice. (This is a skill you must master. Our mission must be complete even if we have to engage in these unpleasantries. Keep your eye on the prize and do not force your hand just because of a bit of discomfort in the technique you may have to use.) He knew that a god was talking to him and knew that he would find that god in the wilderness. I was that god!

I went on to encourage him to seek me in the outdoors and to seek further education from others whom we controlled. He sought spiritual teaching from one of our loyalist but during the instruction The Logos kept trying to whisper to him. It showed in his lack of faith in the work we were trying to do in him yet were succeeding to do in a majority of the other students there.

Many years later he fell under the spell of The Ancient One. This is where the weak demons give up and move on yet this is where our battalion earns its reputation. He moved on to a camp of a man who was strong in his faith and taught his followers on how to effectively talk to The Ancient One. I knew once this occurred my job would take a foul turn. So I returned to the covenant that he and I made all those years ago. He had developed a doubt in the realm of spiritual communication. His fear was of being misled and he made a covenant with the disappointment I placed in his head.

When The Ancient One started to whisper to him I shot my arrows of doubt into the openings of this covenant. I knew I was effective when he wrote in his journal that this teaching on communication was so similar to what he felt in the past that he had doubts in the trustworthiness of this new teacher.

I had counterfeited the work of The Ancient One years before the counterfeit was needed. That access point, through my target's covenant, was enough of a chink for me to get my arrow to pass. Through that opening I was able to continue to have him doubt he ever actually heard from The Ancient One. He began to second-guess all that he heard, believing that it was his own mind that was causing all the direction he heard in his heart. To this day he still cannot discern the voice of The Ancient One from my voice or his own thoughts.

A true devotee of The Ancient One is our biggest challenge. He is one we cannot enter. His heart is occupied by a spirit we cannot overcome so we must use the rules of The Ancient One against his people. Do not fear this; they fall so readily. Just as we have free will they have the freedom to allow in whatever they want to allow in. At this juncture we can easily rely on their animal nature. There are things that they want from life and all we have to do is to show them how to get it from their physical world. They want love; we offer them lust. They want comfort from pain; we offer it to them in the form of a chemical concoction or an animal desire that soothes their heart. We of course do not stop there. Be sure that the first offering ultimately fails to satisfy then offer something more potent. When that does not satisfy they will beg you for something stronger. Soon they will not be capable of living without it and in that despair the voice of The Ancient One is effectively drowned out.

Working with these covenants is the key to making your target ineffective and, if you do your assignment well, can pull your target from the camp of The Ancient One. In time, as you whisper your distortions, you will find a remarkable success. As you encounter another situation where more discouragement is possible you will lean in to whisper and before you draw your breath your target will condemn himself with the words you were going to offer. At this point do not rush in. Let him destroy himself. You still get the credit for clinching the covenant and your target goes on autopilot in the direction you have steered him. Now you can move on to another assignment with only the occasional check up with this one. Feel free to pick at his festering wound when you check in, but be subtle!

Here is the most important thing to remember when doing this work. You will, most likely, be surrounded by the presence of The Ancient One in the form of those angels who did not understand Our King and refused to follow him. Hand to hand with the same level of rank they are not capable of defeating us. And if they are of lesser rank you can push them aside. The trouble is letting your doubts interfere with the battle. In fact, if not called upon they cannot even engage. I love ethics and morality when we can use them to our advantage. So do not be intimidated by their presence. They will certainly make that classic face that says, "Just give me the word, My Lord, and I will move." But your power is secure. Your target has to make the request. The Ancient One will not interfere if the target does not ask for help. If you keep the target occupied he will not even know to whom or for what to ask. Do not be intimidated by their proximity. Just do your duty as described and keep your target moving off the path to the narrow gate. Keep in mind, as residents of our King's physical world they have by nature invited us in. They are born into our camp. The targets we are assigned to overcome have moved, at least partially, from that camp and we are to bring them back. Our advantage is that their nature tends to deliver them to our feet. Whisper well and they will invite you in.

This mission's only difficulty is that our targets are already in the shadow of The Ancient One before we begin our work. Now is the time to refine your skills and apply them with precision and subtlety. Never fear the target. As you will see, if you follow my instruction they will fall at your feet longing for more of what you offer.

OBSERVATION AND TARGET SELECTION

It is imperative that you be able to detect, identify, describe and chart the progression of your enemy. Your predecessors, many led by me, have done a fine job of guiding generations of humans off the path of The Ancient One. So much so that most cannot tell that they have been misdirected. The work has been done so well that even warriors from our camp at times make a misjudgment about their target's status. Be sure you fully study your target and know his allegiances. Full awareness of where they are in our continuum will assure you are using the right tactics. You will soon see that misreading your target and choosing the wrong techniques could be devastating to our cause.

Your key targets will be identified by their actions, both obvious and subtle. Our chief targets are the ones known to the early church as followers of The Way. Today they are called Christians. Many who call themselves Christians or are known to others as Christians are not really that at all. So much the better for us as long as you do not mistake one of ours for one of theirs. Too much pushing of these may cause them to be lost to us.

Our first tool for these targets is to confuse the definition of the terms that define them and to allow the world to see the confusion. We have the advantage of occupying several camps that proclaim their dedication to The Logos without knowing that they are followers of our misinformation. Use these groups already in place to draw in the seeker. Guide them to perceive the restrictions of The Way over the freedom of the path you offer.

For now, we can certainly identify those with no perceived connection to The Ancient One. Allow those to be ministered to by our lesser warriors. You can do your part to help our lesser brethren, in a general way, by giving their targets no encouragement to follow even one of our prescribed paths. Our mission is to keep the unbeliever in unbelief. Barring that, we must keep the seeker seeking our ways and keep the religious away from a relationship with the one who seeks after them.

I will now reveal the whole of the Continuum of Darkness and Light but keep in mind that our primary target is specific. We want to attack those who have put their trust in The Ancient One or The Logos. Yes, we will be working on targets in other categories as well, but those in the darker levels of the continuum we will leave to our King's less talented warriors. The vermin who are lost or confused about what they want and what The Logos wants of them are easy pickings. This type usually poses no trouble until our side makes itself obvious by overplaying their hand. At that point you may have to take over a target because of their advancement on The Continuum of Darkness and Light.

Be aware that all humans have at least a spark of light hidden in them somewhere. This is annoying and I warn you of this so that you are not surprised when one who appears to be in our grasp shows a twitch in the wrong direction. The closer they are to Black on our scale the less likely it will be that you will experience this twitch. On the other side though, the further they are from Black the more work it will require to turn them.

Let us review The Continuum of Darkness and Light in an attempt to better understand whom you will be dealing with and how they might present themselves to you. We will cover the whole Continuum because if you do your assignment as directed you will move your target to the lower levels of this scale and you will still be allowed to play with them there.

The Continuum of Darkness and Light:

Level One: Black. These are rare. They provide much satisfaction, as they willingly do our bidding, but do not count on having this honor. When one is identified at this stage only our most experienced warriors are sent to manipulate their actions. The human leader that will be used in the future to overcome the wretched "Chosen People" will be of this quality. Our King himself will be at the reins of that individual.

Level Two: Dark Gray. These are best described as the devout atheist. They do not believe in The Ancient One because they can only fathom natural causes of their world.

Level Three: Light Gray. Those in this area, such as the determined agnostic, have some of the qualities of those in level two but are more likely at this stage by reasons of choice. They do not want to give up some of the pleasures we have offered them and they know they must if they allowed themselves to believe in a supreme being.

Level Four: Milky Grey. This is the largest and most general group. These are seekers. They have resorted to the admission that there is something "bigger" going on and are followers or teachers of any path other than The Way. Spiritually they have definitive lines of light mixed in with the darkness we covet. Be aware of these lines. They hold the most promise if you can keep your attention, and theirs, on the darker sections of their spiritual swirl.

Level Five: Off White. These are true followers and true teachers of The Way. The last two categories of targets that I describe later in this manual falls into this level.

Level Six: Pure White. We only know of one that held this rank. It was The Logos as a human. We do not expect to see another of this rank but I feel the need to mention it here to be certain our list is complete.

Using the above continuum, the following is a list of targets in the general order of ease: Atheist, Agnostic, Seeker, i.e. (anyone whose interest has been piqued by an experience with a spiritual connection, the follower of any spiritual path, our trained leaders, the followers of one of our spiritual leaders within a Christian denomination.), members of The Way and true teachers and leaders of The Way.

Though this is a typical progression do not assume all will start at one end and progress through each step. One may start anywhere on the list and move forward or backward depending on your cunning. They also may skip steps so be aware. We will be assigned to targets that fall anywhere from seeker and above. Your job is to drive them into doubt and confusion so they fall and remain on the lower levels of the continuum.

What follows is an outline of how to manage the different categories of targets on the continuum. For the most part the only time you will be working with the first two is when you have done your job well and have moved a target backwards down the continuum.

The easy mark, and therefore not a chief concern to us, is the one who does not believe in the possibility of a god. We leave these to others as they have no connection and no relationship with The Ancient One and therefore are low on the continuum. The job of the warriors assigned to this task is to compel them to continue in ignorance. It is quite easy, after all, just by feeding the lusts of their flesh. The mistake that is made with these targets is when, in the excitement of seeing a success, one pushes too hard to watch them fall faster. This common error, overplaying one's hand, will ultimately move the target up on the continuum.

You have been hand picked by me because I trust you will not embarrass me with this mistake. Certainly, it is enjoyable to completely overtake a target but as distress builds, they, and others around them, are more likely to notice that something is afoot. So the key to all you do, my soldier, is patience. Because your objective is best served by being invisible to these targets, camouflage is the key to your success.

You hear the fable often told by these vermin of how a frog placed in cool water upon a lit stove will swim around not knowing it is being cooked until it is too late. Use that tactic with all your targets. Discontentment is their lot so use it. Turn up the heat but do it slowly so they adjust to what you offer them. It will make the successive step in your plan all the more acceptable to your target.

If they show tendencies toward our nature, and if you do your job well they will, exploit that tendency and drive them deep into the worship of Baal or Beelzebub. Just be certain that you give these gods the characteristics your target desires to follow. Our only goal is to keep them from moving in the direction prescribed by The Logos.

The Atheist and Agnostic.

I will cover these two together but they require a variance in the way in which they are handled. The Atheist is one who has no belief in a god and no desire to explore the possibility. For them we promote our standard of physical happenstance. The world came to be by natural causes, the supernatural is not even an option.

The irony of this stance for them is that you, a supernatural being, are influencing them to believe that you cannot exist. Even better is the fact that you, a being created by the Ancient One, are teaching another created being that he is only a lucky spin of a cosmic wheel. Try not to giggle aloud as you lead them into our truths of evolution and random chance.

With the Agnostic you need to be a bit more careful. He has progressed on the continuum and has the potential to believe the possibility of the supernatural. He is open to influence and could become curious. If he gets to that point he becomes a seeker. Use the same proofs you use with the atheist to keep this from occurring. As I stated above, these are often here by choice. They deliberately ignore a gnawing truth to feel as though they can be allowed to indulge in a favorite immorality. Your job is to allow them the comfort of that choice.

If, however, they should evolve toward believing in a supernatural being be sure to guide them to one of our camps. We cannot always prevent the possibility of them pondering a god. Just be sure you become the god they ponder.

The Seeker.

This is the largest group in the continuum. Anyone who has any interest or curiosity that there is something beyond their physical existence should be considered in this category. These (and the following categories) are the ones to which you will be assigned. These are the ones that pose a challenge to our objective. They get to this stage when one of our less competent brothers failed to keep them content in their complacency. These are dangerously close to falling from our Kings grasp but are our finest tool if used properly. They are also the ones I speak of when

I talk about the grease spot on the doorpost of The Logo's infamous narrow gate.

Now we have a reason to step up. Here is someone who has seen enough of the possibility of a supernatural realm that they want to explore it. The reasons for the exploration will be as varied as the targets that choose to explore. Therefore, study them before you embark on a plan to guide them.

Keep in mind that if you have a seeker who you satisfy with a false doctrine they are no longer a seeker. They may remain in the same area on the continuum, embracing a false religion, but they are static and require little maintenance. When working with these keep them satisfied with their new status in one of our religions so they have no need to seek anything else.

Our best tactic here is to rely on the characteristics common to all religions, including The Way, to set the foundation of your target. The focus is to teach them that all religions are really the same and there are many paths to the mountaintop. In your guiding be certain to cover the path to the narrow gate with the weeds and thistles that will keep this target from wanting to explore it. Again, you must study the history of your target. Find the things that you can use to turn them away from seeking The Logos. Make The Way seem incomprehensible or too full of rules or restrictions or un-needed morality or any blockage to the physical needs they have been lead by you to pursue. The Way can certainly be shown to be restrictive. Never allow them to see any freedom in that path.

These targets are exciting. Your work here becomes interesting because you have so many directions in which to lead them. Again the goal is to keep them from that narrow gate but your options are many and exquisite. Here is where your ability to fluidly improvise will become a vital tool. We have, over the centuries, caused to be created so many spiritual paths that any seeker can be nudged toward one of our churches and be fully content with their belief that they are following the truth.

If we properly nurture a new seeker we can take advantage of their nature. This is why I continually instruct on using the physical realm. Most humans do not know the depth of their spiritual existence. They live in the physical world and are influenced by that nature.

Keep them feeling imposed upon when hearing from a true teacher of the Ancient One. They will already have a tendency to seek him but we can appeal to their ego. Use their emotion. Keep them feeling guilty and then judged by those teachers. We want them to be uncomfortable and seeking anything other than what the Ancient One wants them to hear. Our job is to have them seek after things that make them feel good in their primal tendencies and to avoid the unexplored desire of their spirit. Keep them in their flesh! Then when we raise up the teacher we have trained they will flock to those pews.

I just realized a danger in the way I am presenting this information and I want to be sure it does not filter into the way you present options to your targets. Do not focus on the Ancient One or the Logos. Always focus on our King and his desires. We will, at times, have to sway our targets with an option that is similar to the one being offered to them by The Ancient One. Just be sure that your work does not open their eyes to that option.

Now look at all of the choices you can present to your target. Be sure before you take your position in the field that you fully understand at least these two things:

1) The path that is offered by The Ancient One. He calls it a difficult path and so it is. He predicts that few will find it and it is our great pleasure to help fulfill that prophecy.

2) All of the other potential paths, wide and easy, that we can offer to our targets. Just latch on to a list of all the "ism's" we have created over the centuries.

Not only do we have many paths, we have the ability to crisscross and braid these paths so that those who feel no need to be dedicated to a particular path can combine philosophies to suit their, and our, desires.

When you start with one of these targets do not be the one who leads them to any option that has the Logos as part of the plan. Lead them to trails of "love thy neighbor" by showing them that all religions call for this trait. Allow them to do kind things for their neighbor and give money to a local charity. Do not be afraid to allow them to feel needed. They need to know that as long as they do more good than harm all is well. A fine past time in this little game is to see how close you can urge them to a 50/50 split with good and bad. Anything you can do to dilute the meaning of the rulebook offered by The Ancient One will benefit all of us.

Keep them involved in an unorganized hodge-podge of earth based, secular, pseudo-science dogma. Keep them satisfied with finding a system that allows them to do what they want without judgment so that we keep them in our control. If you fail and they seek a deeper knowledge of The Ancient One you are teetering on the brink of failure. It is now the time to be certain you guide them into a denomination of our making with a leader we have installed.

Any path that uses the name of The Logos, and that we invented, falls into this category. You should know the essentials taught and required by The Ancient One and keep your target from believing that they are required or essential. It is even better when you can convince them that other parts of the teachings are essential and that the essentials are not. We have made great headway by causing our followers of our way to argue in public about these essentials. When your target engages in this activity be sure the conversation is painted with much emotion, agitation and anger. Let others see this argument as a way to drive them away from the craziness of these religious adherents. This will make it easier to drive even more away from seeking any course that leads to The Ancient One.

The excitement of having targets in our churches that replicate The Way is dramatic. It makes me heady to think that these are so close to the edge of loss yet my talent will still cause them to fall into our trap. (Remember the grease spot). Oh the satisfaction you will experience when you see their expression at the end of their physical life when their spirit is released, not to their expected heaven, but into utter darkness.

Some people know they are taking a risk with their spiritual choice and are willing to gamble on the outcome. This can be enjoyable as well but so much the better when you have nurtured a belief in them that they are destined for something they believe to be glorious and you secure for them a place in their eternal dungeon. The key to success is to give them enough to believe they are safe but not enough for them to fall into the arms of The Logos.

When working on these targets always return to the basics. Our techniques need to remain simple. Use their fear of the loss of control or autonomy. Be sure that if they are going to follow this closely to the edge that we keep in the front of their minds the need to be in charge, to be right and to be pushing their agenda toward the others around them. Let them use their strong will and leadership to do our work for us.

Lead one of these well and they will lead two more. If this trend can continue they will cause the destruction of countless others without you even breaking a sweat. Once misled they will discard out of hand the doctrines essential to The Way believing they interfere with and dilute the truth.

Our Leaders of Our Way

These are the people we have trained to be leaders of misinformation of The Way.

Often these are accidental, but it is always in your interests to look for likely candidates. When, in the last section, I talked of guiding your targets to one of our churches, it is to these leaders I refer. Again, we are teetering on the edge with these so you must be very deliberate with every one of your actions. Though you may not yet believe the importance of my recurring statement you must stick to the basics. The techniques that are most effective have been used for centuries and have shown consistent, reproducible results. Appeal to their animal nature: Pride, ego, sexual and financial lust, longing for respect and adoration, etcetera.

Our key target in this group is the person of influence. We want to focus on the charismatic, the scholar, the teachers, those people who have, or will have, a large sphere of influence. We want them to build a following so we can control their circle with only the work of controlling them. Those who become followers of these leaders will still need monitoring and whispers but if you control the leader you have sway over the crowd. This will allow one to do the work of many and it will free up more of our limited troops to work on more delicate targets.

Our first line of defense when someone shows potential to lead a church is to be the ones who set them up as a person of influence. We have spent generations working with this tactic and it has always served us well.

Man's pride is our tool. Some want to be teachers for the glory their parishioners bestow upon them. They crave the adoring looks and comments from the pews. Some do it for the financial gain. They can be taught to stretch the meaning of their scripture to appeal to the hearts of their audience. Let the crowd send their money as long as they never see what the actual scripture reads. You have all read that document; misdirection is vital.

This is where the collaboration of warriors becomes so critically important. There will always be those who only seek after the spiritual out of a compulsion in society that he does so. That person can be used to lean into the teacher to say they contribute much to the church but are offended by some of what they hear from the pulpit. They might be lead to say that they do not want to hear of things like sin and they know of many others who have been offended. Those others do not want to make a scene but it has been made known that if they are continually made uncomfortable while listening to the teacher they will take their affection, and money, elsewhere. So the teacher, who mostly wants the support of his congregation, can be made to fear the loss so much that he changes his teaching to things that will not offend. This offense can be used well on both sides of the battle. We must whisper into the hearts of our targets how the words of scripture are offensive to their sensibilities and we must whisper into the mind of the teacher that he dare not risk offending the congregation. We do not always have this perfect set up but it occurs much more frequently now than it ever has before.

Another fine target that will have multiple rewards is the one in leadership who never fully found the complete path. On the surface they are strong members of the church community with high moral standards. But because they have not fully brought themselves under the authority and covering of The Logos they are not protected. They usually have many openings by which we can gain access. I like to take my time with these. Lull them, nurture them, and pull the trigger when many are watching. Oh how sweet the fall when it is from dizzying heights! (And even better when they chose to jump willingly and many follow).

It is easy for these humans to cling to their animal natures and we do well to exploit them. They want fame. So we offer it to them through our channels of misdirection. Let them teach many as long as what they teach is in line with our direction and not that of The Ancient One. (Of course, it is best if we can make it seem like the direction of The Ancient One through our camouflage. Let them believe they are holy by teaching them improperly) A dangerous course but oh so delectable when necessary, is to let a leader teach the truth, as The Logos sees it, but then to bring this leader down in front of his adherents. At that stage many will walk away from the faith in disillusionment or disgust and seek another course. Your follow up is to give them that other course.

Bring this leader of others down through one of his covenants: lust, pride, ego or anger. Before you make this attempt you must know your target. Use whatever weaknesses he has displayed and deliver your whispers. Be certain that he is made to believe that what he seeks is perfectly normal for one in his position. That way when it takes him down, he will falter wondering what happened. Though, with this sort of attack you will gain many who fall from faith, be sure not to leave your first target on his own. His return to The Logos could cause you much harm. Keep him going in the direction on which you started him. As you may know there is nothing more satisfying than pulling one from the arms of The

Logos and watching his fall all the way to his bitter end. But remember this! If your target was at all close to The Ancient One, when he falls you must keep feeding him the physical pleasures. To pull him completely into despair will only have him seeking a spiritual relief. We want his seeking for relief to always be physical. Allow him to have joy in his lusts. If you are one to feel uncomfortable allowing joy then you will fail. Let them be happy as long as it is a happiness based on our direction. At this stage we must never allow him to be reminded of any of the flirtations of The Logos. If one comes up whisper to him about the let down and drive that stake deep. Do not allow for spiritual contemplation. Physical, physical, physical!

Followers of The Way

We have limits on how close we can get to these but there are still tactics we can use. I will show you how to use your tools and launch your weapons to penetrate their defenses. Those of you charged with this population need to be diligent and vigilant. You must monitor them constantly for an appropriate opening. When they twitch, we pounce. They doubt, we encourage that doubt. They get tired or frustrated we whisper the temptation, the drug, into their heart with the assurance that they have earned and deserve a break due to all the hardships and misunderstandings that surround them in their life.

(Hardships and misunder-standings hopefully introduced, and nurtured by you.) Use them one against another for the victory we seek. Learn to work with other warriors to have those around them to compound their distress Our plan is the same with these as with others but we must be much more precise and detailed.

True Leaders of The Way.

This will be your most frustrating assignment. These are the ones who most understand the needs and requirements of The Ancient One and who, for the most part are willing to bow to these requirements.

Do not go into this one unaware. The only defense against us any follower of the Ancient of Days has is the power he grants them and that they accept. He grants this power freely so our only tactic against it is misdirection and subterfuge to prevent acceptance. One who is fully aware of this offering from The Ancient One is not penetrable. All you can do is to watch for his missteps and do your best to capitalize on them. Attempt to use past covenants to seal some sort of deal but hold no illusions. Once a man fully understands what the Ancient One offers, we have no quarter, no hold. If you are the one in charge when a man reaches this point woe to you!

We must endeavor to discredit and destroy this leadership. They will be held to a higher standard and watched by everyone—especially the doubters. If you can discredit them the job of our warriors working with their congregations will be all the easier. (Again, work together. If it is apparent that the leader is getting set up for the fall, be sure the congregant you are working on is being set up to be devastated by that fall.)

When you take out a well-known leader you effectively disrupt that church, cause division in other believers and give non-believers and seekers many reasons to mistrust that now hypocritical group. One fall counts as many victories for Our King.

You will be repelled often by a true leader's submission to The Logos. If you have not yet experienced this phenomenon be strong. When one of these calls upon the authority of The Logos to bind you, you will be bound. It is unnerving and disorienting. If that should be your destiny your head will clear and when it does return to your post. Do not allow your anger or frustration to overcome you. You must lie in wait and offer him ways to feed his flesh. It will be the hardest thing you will ever do but enough of these men have fallen to our work that we can always justify the idle time as we wait for an opportunity. So you will have to be patient. You cannot be off tempting and tormenting others because the opportunities opened by these leaders are few and far between. If you happen to be elsewhere when the opening comes your only chance may be lost.

Use your time well by sending other humans to try to wear them down or to appeal to their deep-seated instincts as humans. Just as I insist you should all work with each other you should always use these targets one against another.

A grand focus for a church leader is his family. Encourage disillusionment and discord with his wife and children. When his congregation sees his family fall away from his influence doubt can be placed in their minds as to his worthiness to be followed.

The urge in us all is to cause the physical world to crush the life from this target so that we can move on to another. This, however, often creates a martyr. Not necessarily by their dying doing the work of The Ancient One but by the admiration he has from his congregation. It is better to watch and find a chink than to send him to The Logos and have his followers cemented all the more through the sympathy of the circumstances of his death.

Our only hope is to affect his congregation and lead them off so that he loses heart. The implementation of ideas that cause a man to lose heart is a fine goal. If that can be achieved then you can get a toehold. Find some situation that can be perceived as a scandal and do your best to exploit it among the populace and his followers. Break him down from without if it cannot be done from within.

With these it is critical that we work together. If we cannot cause one of these to lose heart or fall into our trap our last objective is to discredit them and make them ineffective for the kingdom of The Ancient One. Work with other teams who have a seeker who is still easily influenced to our side. If we can discredit our target in front of our comrade's target that one will be less likely to ever cross over.

No matter the level of your target or those around them our goal is simple: more humans to miss, or be ignorant of, the Narrow Gate. Work together toward this goal and our battalion's successes will be assured.

Never let it be otherwise.

Tools and Devices of An Effective Warrior.

The easiest and most effective tool to use against your target is their human nature. Keep them focused on their animal desires and your target will do much of your work for you. I have mentioned some of the aspects of their nature before and later in this chapter I will cover many others.

The devices you have at your disposal to exploit their nature are things like mistrust, deceit, misdirection, misrepresentation, lying and trickery. All of these terms in their world have come to mean a guiding away from truth. I use them in their proper definition of directing people away from the unreasonable expectations of the Ancient One's directives. We must show them that all of His expectations are unreasonable and that they should rely on the desires of their animal nature to give them purpose.

It should be apparent to you by now that most of the targets you will be engaging live in their physical world and do not fully comprehend the spiritual aspect of their nature. Keep them in the dark on this topic. When they experience a connection to the spiritual they have a natural tendency to apply the characteristics of the physical world to it. If they happen to experience a joy caused by a glimmer of their spirit be certain to always redirect their minds to the physical aspect of that pleasure. If they are able to connect their physical pleasure with the intent of The Ancient One to provide that pleasure your position will be nearly impossible to reclaim.

If this should occur be certain not to attack by trying to discredit the pleasurable feeling. That is too direct and too obvious. Always dig into your arsenal to find another angle to distract them. Use a job stress or a relationship confrontation. This is effective in two ways. It causes their bliss to evaporate and it causes them to blame the intruder for the loss of that bliss. Now you have an opening back to the physical. If spun well this opens a whole new line of pain and distraction and keeps them from looking for the thing that sent them the joy.

Do you see how improvisation is the key to winning the battle? If I gave you a numerical list of what to do to win over your target all it would take is a counter move by our enemy to disrupt your chronological movement. If you can bend and flex into the fight you can keep up your end and then return to your level of progression when the move is countered. This is chess not hop-scotch.

You will do well to emulate your leader. I so fluidly speak my will into the minds of these creatures and the authority in which I speak increases my success. Tell your target anything, but do it with authority and he will believe it. Our King is the Father of Lies. Do your work so that you are worthy of such a title.

These creatures are base and primal. It is so easy to distract them by calling on their natural urges. Hunger or fatigue can lure them away from a whisper from The Ancient One. A call of a chore forgotten can distract them from their intended communication with The Logos. Remember our targets have a leaning toward The Ancient One. It is as though He is planted somehow in their consciousness. We must, then, be certain that whatever He whispers is being overcome by what our target thinks he needs.

If your target is lonely and in need of love do not allow him to fall toward the Logos; lead him to desire love from a physical source. Focus not on the spiritual fulfillment they unknowingly crave but on the physical release provided by the pursuit of a lustful relationship. Always justify in their minds why they deserve to follow this course. Afterwards, and this is true of all direction you provide, make them feel the condemnation of their fall. This will cause them to go deeper into despair and require a more powerful drug for relief. Then whisper the words they long to hear. "You are suffering so. Why not indulge yourself in that drug again." Then subtly keep up the spiral. The goal is to make them feel so guilty that they can no longer, with a clear conscience, seek help or counsel. When you and their thoughts are the only voices in their head you will be in complete control.

Because the focus of this volume is upon the creatures that have at least a cursory allegiance to The Logos the most interesting and at times the most challenging tool is the Rule Book of The Ancient of Days.

We have worked for centuries to cast a cloud of doubt over the veracity of this book. Take advantage of that work. In this book The Ancient of Days tells his stories but we are just as fanciful in our story telling as he. When using this tool leave out the unimportant parts and focus on what is available for you to reach your goal. Keep in the forefront of your target's mind all of the variations of interpretation that can be used when reading this book. Whenever he is reading on his own be sure to whisper to him how what he is reading can justify the things you want to lead him into. Be sure he interprets the concepts in a way that keeps him on your side.

For example: When Ezekiel writes of the wheel within a wheel use your targets history to see this as a description of a space vehicle. Encourage him to see that life on this earth was planted by some more intelligent being from a galaxy far, far away. Then when he looks at the stars it is easier for him to think of which one has the other inhabited planets around it instead of when or if it was all created.

You can pick nearly any story from this book and spin it toward the covenants and physical urges of your target. Look how easy it has been to convince many targets they have permission to indulge in polygamy because many of the early fathers of Israel had multiple wives. If they dabble in this book only reveal to them what you want them to know for your advantage. Be cautious, however. Remember even our King was pushed back when he used these words against The Logos. We cannot win when The Logos uses his word against us even if he is doing it through one of our intended targets.

We will never have to face the Logos directly or any adversary of that caliber but we must still be careful not to become cavalier when using these words against a minion of The Ancient One. If they are aware of what it really contains we too can be pushed back. But here is our good news; most are blissfully unaware.

In earlier days our best tactic was keeping the book out of the hands of the common believers. Then all we had to do was to work with our advance targets to be sure they were passing along partial, and ineffective, details. As long as they had a misunderstanding of the book or a personal reason to mislead their congregation we had the upper hand. Leaning on tradition and man made religion is still a noble device. As time grows short we must use those devices even more. The Ancient's book states that men will fall away from him and want only to have their ears tickled. I say we must use this promise to our advantage. Set up your false teachers and tickle away!

Remember; even though you will not all have highly visible targets your job is to make these vermin ineffective for their cause. All mistrust, misdirection and misunderstanding is encouraged. And, if you do have a target that is responsible to a church take him out. I do not mean kill him but let him teach many poorly or have him fall to one of his covenants in front of his followers. In this way you work on the one but affect to your advantage the many.

A prime example of how to use this book against them is the account of Our King challenging The Ancient One over the loyalty of one of his servants. As I stated in the introduction our King has access to the Ancient of Days and he uses that access to work his plan. We may not understand why he does what he does but nonetheless he does what he will.

During one of those meetings our King accuses one of The Ancient's beloved and that one, Job, is defended by The Ancient One. Lucifer is given access to this one to prove that the only reason he is loyal is because he is perfectly protected.

How this ends up is hardly the point. The point is that as it is told, it shows the reader that their God has all the flaws they have themselves. It also shows their misunderstanding of the spiritual relationships we all enjoy but they cannot see physically. I love to use this book to show people that The Ancient and

Lucifer must be co-equal because our King is able to entice The Ancient One into a wager. Again, do not focus on anything but the fact that The Creator allows his loyal and loved servant to go through immense suffering just so He can attempt to win a bet with Lucifer. In the end, as I see it, Job suffers the lost of everything he loved and enjoyed only because of the pride of his God.

Use the book to always cast doubt, to always confuse, to always misdirect. The beauty is that there is no way that the limits of the human brain could ever fully tell the story. As it is written it is easy to convince the reader that The Ancient One has the same ego and Pride that is part of all mankind. And that He wants to be worshipped because of his pride and not due to any sort of self proclaimed intrinsic worth.

You can see how easy it is to use the known qualities of your target to cast doubt on the book that they claim to relish and follow without question. Our job is to open up their mind to question everything. Alone they are no challenge to us and even in groups they have no real power without the authority of The Logos. Keep them from that knowledge.

I am overjoyed by the story of the 7 sons of Sceva for the way it turned to my favor. I recount the story to point out a valuable lesson, however, if not handled with determination or if not followed through this sort of victory can turn against us.

This story will show you how to use the religious leaders who do not properly follow The Logos. These are the ones when properly nurtured that can be placed into our churches. As you know, the men who came to their patient to attempt to remove me from his body called upon The Logos and one of His primary apostles but they had no connection with the Logos themselves. They wanted to take the glory of the healing as their own. When they called out to me to leave they mentioned the Logos and the Apostle Paul. I said that I knew the Apostle and I knew the Logos but who are you? I then did as they requested. I left the body of my target and pummeled them physically. They left the building torn, tattered, bleeding and in great fear. I then returned into the body of my target and continued my work in and through him.

These stories are in their rulebook of The Ancient One and they offer wonderful examples of how to use His book against the believers of The Logos. We do that with misdirection.

The book is leading the reader to believe that he might have the ability to push us out of our rightful dwelling in the heart of a man. We, then, must redirect the reader to see it differently. Use fear. Whisper the thought, "I do not want to mess with that sort of thing. I will just let the spiritual realm be." Use doubt. Whisper, "This can not be a real account. Demons do not even exist. This guy was just crazy and in that state of mind had the use of strength we all have hidden somewhere."

Or better yet, do as I did. Let people believe they have some sort of power but keep them from stepping into a relationship with the son of The Ancient One. Our perfect tool is to allow them to know the beginning of what we know. The Ancient One exists. Just keep their hearts from the rest.

We loose no one to the profession that there is a creator. Let them languish in that thought but do not let them spend too much time thinking it through. They believe in The Ancient One? Fine, but do not allow them to explore getting close to him. Keep him, in the minds of your target, far off and unreachable. Whisper "He is an old man in a rocking chair who started the world spinning and is waiting to see how it all turns out." Then cause pain and introduce havoc into your subject's life and whisper "See, if he cared he would keep you from this. He is of no help or consequence. He is in fact just a player in the cosmic scheme of things."

Keep up the image we have put into the stories of the early intellectual communities. That the many gods of their world struggle and fight with one another for control and there is no way for the gods or the people to know the outcome. Convince them that they will struggle because they are alone. My experience tells me they will valiantly push but as I said before they have no power when they are alone.

The desire to do battle is built in to them but so is the desire to fight solo. When they do this they will tire and fail. So then we work effectively within their discouragement. As they fight and do not see any help we remind them that The Ancient One either does not care or has no power. He is just watching what is happening with a curious interest hoping for the best.

These vermin, early in the continuum, have the nearly universal tendency to believe that they are the Supreme Being on this planet. Use their natural tendency of supremacy against them. They picture themselves evolved higher than the rest of the animals and because of their larger brain have reached the point of almost divine authority over he Earth. Of course since we do not want to reveal ourselves to them they would assume as much. But because of their natural tendency we can whisper greatly disruptive ideas into their heads. Let them think that The Ancient One works as they would in their world. When he demands worship let them believe it is due to pride and arrogance. When he tells them of their sin let them feel betrayed and utter "who do you think you are demanding perfection from me while you sit up there on your high horse looking down at me. I thought you were a god of love…" Be sure that when they look to a god, if they look at all, they do it from the perspective of how they would do things if they were in charge. So much misdirection is available from this perspective.

We want mostly to have the minions hear this from their leaders and teachers at the pulpit. You have done well when you have placed these ideas into a leader of a congregation. Let him teach and spread our word into the crowd. Let them teach that his followers are to be gods or are the dominant beings and all have the qualities of deities. This works like a virus and before you know it nearly everyone is infected and ready to fall. They long to be important and on top of the food chain. Just keep an eye on your target if he is in this crowd and starts to show resistance to the message. If that should happen it is time to rely heavily on the rest of our devices as listed below.

PASSIVITY

These creatures are by nature rebellious for the reasons mentioned previously. If it is not their idea they are inclined to resist. One of our most effective tools is to hinder or shut down communication between them and The Ancient One. Pulling them into a state of passivity is a fine tool. If you are needling them consistently and slowly, but quietly, wearing them down, when the time comes for them to pray your subtle whispers of "that seems pointless", or "you can do it later", should result in their saying "Do I really need to do this" or "This can just wait. I will do it after dinner". Even if they pick up the duty again later, and most of them will not, it will not have the same passion or the same impact as if they did it when The Ancient One directed them. Keep them occupied with other details of their physical life and dull them to the effect that their talking with The Ancient One can cause. In fact, keep them believing that prayer is a boring obligation; a tired monolog with something that may or may not even be listening.

If one of their brethren talks to them of the trouble they are having, usually due to one of your compatriots doing their job well, and if it looks as though they may start to pray, urge them to wait for a different time. A time that is more private ("You do not want to make a spectacle of yourself in this public area") or more conducive to their short attention span (Just before bed when all is quiet and you can lull them off to sleep before anything effective happens). Use anything, but be certain they put it off until later so that you can change that into not at all.

MANIPULATION

We have worked since the beginning of time to use our truths to divert our targets from a connection with The Ancient One. Raising up a leader in the church to speak these truths to the congregation is a noble course.

Take any one of our flamboyant evangelists for example. We put him in a position of power to lead from a platform of trust. It matters not whether he believes what he preaches or if he is truly on our side and is using the enemy for his own gain. The benefit is two fold. He misleads his followers so they do not truly connect and his antics turn away seekers so that they see this belief system for the circus that we know it to be.

Combining the manipulation of the rulebook with the antics of one of our teachers is always a good combination. The rulebook of The Ancient One states, for example, "The love of money is the root of all kinds of evil". But we have our evangelist preaching that if you give to his ministry The Ancient One will bless you 30, 60, 100-fold. We have our targets finance our work through their greed and their love of money. Keep the congregant's eyes on the preacher and off of the rulebook and you only have to work with the one man to misdirect the whole crowd.

Now turn him into a yelling clown with big hair and questionable antics and anyone who accidentally sees him will be repulsed from his behavior. It will now be easy to whisper to them of the lunacy of this religion so that they will not want to be in proximity to it. Let them abuse the alleged gifts of The Ancient One so they look asinine and the job just gets easier. To his congregation he is one to follow but we are leading them all astray. To the casual observer he is a lunatic who discredits the whole idea of The Ancient One's plan.

Whatever we do we want to avoid allowing them to really experience the offerings of The Ancient One. The sufferings, yes, but never the joy. We want to encourage doubt, fear, anger and confusion, anything that will shatter faith. Remember, they cannot see The Ancient One, only his effects. Keep them believing in natural causes and coincidence.

MISDIRECTION

In everything we do we have to appeal to the human nature. They want what they want and will accept any information that will keep them on their chosen path. Leading people away from what The Ancient One wants of them will require a mastery of this art form.

Consider this line painted on the wall of the office of one of my targets. "Henceforth, I take my stand that my physical body is now and forevermore shall be the Temple of the Most High." You will see its parallel in a scriptural quote. But notice how it is subtly bent to conform to my need in my target. She attends a church that claims to follow The Way but, as we have directed, it contends that each member is part of their own divinity. (Our King's original tactic is still effective to this day.)

Take notice where she placed the capitol letters in this quote. Her physical body becomes a Temple with a capital T. Just like the Most High. This is their way of acknowledging The Ancient One. She has equated herself with being a god. Many will see this line and find it innocuous. Once it is in their head it is your job to seal it into their heart to cause their desire for that outcome.

LUST

This is a most universal tool. Many think it only is useful in regards to sex but our targets will lust after anything. It is related to covetousness. I have had the lust for buying books about The Logos work for me when the target was doing it for the lust of spending money that he was to be saving for other financial obligations. I made the books ineffective as they sat upon his shelf as he despaired over how to reclaim the money spent so he could by groceries.

PRIDE

This is one of our major tools. Use it often. It is the bedrock of all the rest of our work with emotions. I have been speaking of this tool throughout my treatise. Capitalize on their longing for divinity, recognition, fame, fortune and their desire for solo achievement. Appeal to your target's pride and watch as a plethora of doors open to you.

DEPRESSION AND DISPAIR

There are several human emotions that we can rely upon even if your work did not cause their onset. Always take advantage of them when you see them. These are the ones where you whisper your wisdom to cause a target to sin then whisper what a wretch they are. Then, when they are really low because of your work, you encourage them to delve into the same activity again. Just keep circling until they collapse.

ANGER AND RAGE

There are depictions of The Logos being angry in their scripture. Use this. For some it can be a cause to doubt His veracity. For others, who depict it as "a righteous anger", we can use it to give them cause to allow their own anger to build and then give them a passage to justify their rage. Anger is never enough but it is the foundation for you to build upon.

FEAR

Once they believe that you exist you might employ the tactic of letting them see you everywhere. This has its concerns but a mastery of style can keep their focus on you at the exclusion of the Ancient of Days. This device has many uses because these animals fear much. It is your job to understand their personalities and uncover their covenants so that you can control that fear for your gain.

COVETOUSNESS

This one is almost as easy as pride and can be used in conjunction with lust. People want possession, power, prestige and recognition. Develop these fleshly desires to a lust for each and they will be covenants that will allow you access even if your target's status on The Continuum moves against you. Satisfaction in their physical world is found by having things that equate to status. Drive your target to want more than others have and then even more still. Then hide the fact that the emptiness inside them can never be filled.

DECEIT

Our King is called "The Father of Lies" by the opposition. This is a bit of a stretch. Their unholy dislike of Lucifer causes them to use the hypocritical title. But they do get to this opinion because of his mastery of our device. It works best when you take the words of the enemy and bend them, or omit parts, to cause the effect we desire. Let them believe they love each other as long as they still back stab and gossip. We all know from our experience that The Ancient Ones rules are farfetched and unreasonable. This is where we can set the record straight in the minds of our targets. Work smarter not harder. Save your effort when you can use them against themselves. I have alluded to this often but as long as they co-mingle we should be working with each other to set up their friction and conflict.

Let them believe all that they do should be credited to themselves. Do not allow them to see the work of The Ancient One in their situation. Self glory at all costs! We have taught, and they must believe, that all of their spiritual progression comes from the work they do. Let them believe that what will make them whole is to do more good work than bad deeds. Because many already hold to this premise be sure that your target has the opportunity to confide in one of those. They will then be comforted by one who they trust but who will deceive them. It is better for you if the one who leads them astray actually believes what they say in their counsel to your target.

INSECURITY

The human has a tendency for self-doubt and false assumption. Our goal is to capitalize on this trait. This goes along with using their intellect in harmony with their emotions. It is easier by far to get a fingernail under a sour emotion but once there be sure to control the intellects approach to the topic. Let them believe that the reason there is no response to their prayer is because of the thing they did about which they are feeling guilty. Better still if you caused them to head down the path that lead to the infraction.

Once you have set this up you can go to and fro and cause the emotional roller coaster effect that will topple them. Lead them to make a move that is against what they are trying to believe. Once they do remind them it was wrong and urge their intellect to beat them up for it. If they start to pray for forgiveness be certain you instill guilt or shame. Let them know that they are worthless in the eyes of The Ancient One and that he does not want to hear their whining. They are lost and there is nothing anyone can do for them. Then during this despair lead them again into temptation.

INTELLECT

This goes along with the building of religious ceremony and conventions. When we use their rulebook against them we must be certain to mould it to the current context or to spin it to be outside of why it was written. They must never be allowed to see any simplicity in the Ancient Ones calling. We must always push for them to add to his requests. We want them to quibble over inconsequential details but this is to no avail if they agree on the major points of The Logo's desire. So for those who claim The Way as their own but are not yet so, lead them to quibble. Those who truly follow His tenants need to be drawn away with their intellect. Confuse and confound them; whisper discouragement into their happy little lives; get them to wonder if God is listening then set up the stage for a covenant that will allow you access.

These humans also have a curious desire to do good things. Well, let them. But be sure that their reason for doing these things will lead to self-glory or self-recognition. The end result must be for the thanks they desire not the selfless reasons desired by The

Ancient One. Let them stew if thanks and adoration are not heaped upon them. Let them find joy in helping a friend who is down but whisper to them how ungrateful their friend is if they do not heap praise upon them. Let them obsess over the lack of appreciation or recognition they receive. Always hint that they are right to do good but that they should always be disdainful when not praised for it.

Use their intellect to defend their unorthodox positions. Let them feel justified with comments such as, "We do not need to be born again. We got it right the first time". Make the pet phrases of The Way be a bane and foolishness to the everyday citizen. Intelligent people do not need the crutch of religion. Allow the terminology of The Ancient One to become distasteful or arcane in the minds of the masses. Do not allow your target to explore the Rule Book; just turn them away to our higher pursuits. Never let their intellect be a part of their looking at the rulebook of The Ancient One.

MISDIRECTION

Our side has created many doctrines that are loyally followed, that contradict teachings of the Logos. Some even counterfeit those teachings. How many similarities can we pack into how many different religions and still steer people from The Ancient One? Look around and the answer is apparent. We hold more to our sway than The Creator of these vermin Himself!

CAMOUFLAGE

This is the key to our success. When using all of the listed tools and devices we must at all times remain hidden. If your target sees the work you are doing as coming from us he will dig in and defend himself. We have overcome this type and it is not easy. Do not expose yourself. Be aware also of those around your target who may be sensitive to the spiritual world. If they see your tactics they will alert their brother. You still may be able to hold on to your position but why risk it? Remain in the shadows.

Use all of our devices to cover your tracks. Cause guilt but let them believe it comes from within. Better still make them believe someone of their circle is trying to make them feel guilty and then cause a rift between them. Divide and conquer.

This may seem obvious but there have been warriors,
accustomed to working with those on the lowest scales of The Continuum, who forget the difference between those who follow willingly and those who resist. With the latter we must not be apparent. Always use one or many, of the listed devices to knock your target off of their path to The Ancient One. They must know these feelings are justified and

come from themselves especially if they are provided by you. Never allow your justified pride to show through just so you can take credit for their fall in front of them. Do the work in secret and enjoy the look in their eyes when they find out their eternal mistake.

Both intellect and emotion can be dangerous in our quest. Do not enter into your work lightly. As strong as these can be for our cause they also have the potential of being effective for our enemy. We exploit the emotion of fear, anger and lust. We dance around the emotion of joy and love. If you can use joy to exploit a covenant forbidden by The Ancient One then do so, but be ever vigilant of how these things can turn against you in this battle.

Applying the Tactics

Once you have worked this battle plan effectively it is important that you review the tactics from time to time. If you start to lose control of one of your targets use this tome as a review and a reminder of the basics.

We must always work together. Know what your neighboring compatriot is up to in the target that interacts with yours.

Always remain hidden. Let them see only your device to draw them away and never the fact that it is a device. Whisper to them but do it in such a way that they believe it was their idea. Lead them without them being aware of being led.

Focus on the inflamed physical world they inhabit. It offers so much to draw upon. And the longer we rule that world the more we will invent to be drawn upon. Even without your help they will stumble and slog through their daily existence. Whether you cause it or not, capitalize on it.

It is an easy task to whisper doubt into their minds. If there is a god why do I suffer? Do not focus on the suffering of others; keep their eyes on themselves. Let them believe that a loving god would never let such and such happen. Do not let them focus on their part of their fallen existence. Blame it all on a far away god and not on their fatal choices or our involvement. If they see those things they will begin to rally around a solution that focuses on a possibility we do not want them to see. Namely that they are weak and they need to rely on some strength outside of themselves.

Feed them with doubt. Let them see suffering but let that suffering cause distress in their belief in a devine protector. Better still; let them feel suffering to prove they have no protector. Use all the power you have to focus their attention on pain and keep them from bliss. Focus on fear to keep them from comfort. Focus on horror to keep them from contentment. Give them every reason to doubt the Logos and even more reason to shun those who have fallen into that fabled love affair. Make that relationship and the people who have fallen for it appear weak, foolish and wrong-headed.

It is easy to stir up all these emotions even in a strong believer. The trick is to keep the drip of pain upon them until they feel despair. If they are inclined to pray for help tighten the screws to keep them away from that resource. Whisper to them the fact that if prayer worked they certainly would not be suffering. Let them know, and then make them believe, that there is no one to hear their cries; at least no one who cares. They must rely on themselves only. Then slowly allow them to realize that they have nothing with which to save themselves. Offer this not to the point of their seeking a savior but to the point of despair. Then, within that despair, offer them your drug of salvation.

This part must be slow. The Logos has a way of infiltrating the hearts of these people when they are suffering. Before you cast them off as being unable to help themselves you must be certain you have convinced them that they are alone. Do not give them hope that there is anything out there that can help them except the medication you offer from their physical world. Then medicate them: Sex, alcohol, drugs or any physical lust that they can draw upon for temporary pleasure. Afterward you can whisper the reminder of their failures and make them feel guilty for indulging in that pleasure. The magic is in using that guilt to call them right back to the same drug. May the circle be unbroken!

Let them know that faith fulfilled requires proof and there is no proof of this invisible god they claim to follow.

So in conclusion take advantage of the following:

*They are weak.

*They have nothing without the defense of the Logos—keep them from that at all costs.

*They want the easy way, give it to them.

*Give them the general items common to all of our religions but keep them from the specific narrow gate. Let them feel good about love and tolerance but stir up offense about any mention of one way to a god.

*Feed their flesh; their animal instincts. In fact keep them believing they are nothing more than animals and allow them the permission they need to wallow there.

*Feed their human desires for fame, pride, jealousy, covetousness, depression, despair, and so on.

Keep them so focused on these troubles that they cannot see or do not seek the alleged promises of their God. In this way you can become their god!!!

PART TWO

A CHRISTIAN CALL TO ARMS

UNDERSTANDING OUR ENEMY

The Cunning Dragon tells his proselytes that our weaknesses are many and our strengths are few. Part of the effective strategy of this enemy is using truth and bending it or using partial truth with enough authority to get us to believe it as the whole truth. We should start with our areas of agreement with the Cunning Dragon

Compared to this enemy we are weak and we can agree that our weaknesses are many. For Christians to take on this enemy alone would be a total disaster.

We live in a fallen world and everything that has been separated from the proper relationship with God can be a temptation to us. These temptations become an opening for us to be overcome by our enemy. The Cunning Dragon also states that our strengths are few. This too is true, but here is where we draw our encouragement. Our strengths may be few in number but each one, used as designed, is more powerful than our enemy.

One of our strengths is our foreknowledge of the enemy. Just as The Cunning Dragon is teaching his devotees about us, we too need to know what drives them. By studying what the Bible says about Satan we will better understand the angels who follow him. Their tactics and motivation are the same.

In the book of Ezekiel, we have an account of who Lucifer was as an angel of God and how his pride changed him.

"Thus says the Lord God:
'You were the seal of perfection,
Full of wisdom and perfect in beauty.
You were in Eden, the garden of God;
Every precious stone was your covering:
The sardis, topaz, and diamond,
Beryl, onyx and jasper,
Sapphire, turquoise, and emerald with gold.
The workmanship of your timbrels and pipes
Was prepared for you on the day you were created.
You were the anointed cherub who covers;
I established you;
You were on the holy mountain of God;
You walked back and forth in the midst of fiery stones.
You were perfect in your ways from the day you were created,
Till iniquity was found in you.
By the abundance of your trading
You became filled with violence from within,
And you sinned;
Therefore I cast you out as a profane thing
Out of the mountain of God;
And I destroyed you, O covering cherub,
From the midst of the fiery stones.

Your heart was lifted up because of your beauty;
You corrupted your wisdom for the sake of your splendor;
I cast you to the ground,
I laid you before kings,
That they might gaze at you.' "
(Ezekiel 28: 12-17)

Lucifer was overcome by his beauty and allowed corruption to seep in through his pride. By studying Satan, it becomes apparent that the tool he uses the most effectively is the thing that brought him down.

Isaiah gives more detail of Lucifer's fall into Satan. Notice the references to his prideful desires.

'How you are fallen from heaven,
O Lucifer, son of the morning!
How you are cut down to the ground,
You who weakened the nations!
For you have said in your heart:
'I will ascend into heaven,
I will exalt my throne above all the stars of God;
I will also sit on the mount of the congregation
On the farthest side of the north;
I will ascend above the heights of the clouds,
I will be like the most high.'
Yet you shall be brought down to sheol,
To the lowest depths of the pit."
(Isaiah 14:12-15)

The battle that ensues in heaven that cast Lucifer out is summed up in Revelation.

"And a war broke out in heaven: Michael and his angels fought with the dragon; and the dragon and his angels fought, but they did not prevail, nor was a place found for them in heaven any longer. So the great dragon was cast out, that serpent of old, called the Devil and Satan, who deceives the whole world; he was cast to the earth, and his angels were cast out with him."
(Revelation 12:7-9)

Though Satan is a created, fallen being his desire is for the world to believe that he is equal to God and worthy of worship. He attempts to deceive you into believing that he truly has the thing that you want. Satan's authority comes first from the fall in the garden and second from us allowing him access when we give in to the desires of our flesh. He has no access to us without us first allowing an opening. As we deal with those openings, whether intentional or unintentional, we struggle and at times feel overwhelmed and ill equipped. When that happens consider the following:

"Those who see you will gaze at you,
And consider you, saying:
'Is this the man who made the earth tremble,
Who shook kingdoms,
Who made the world as a wilderness

And destroyed its cities
Who did not open the house of his prisoners?' "
(Isaiah 14:16-17)

The above passage from Isaiah continues to speak of Satan after his final defeat. When reading the line "Is this the man…?", think of the scene in "The Wizard of Oz" when Toto pulls back the curtain to reveal that great and powerful Oz was merely a man with a microphone. Once revealed we will say, "This guy? Really? We were afraid of him?" That is part of his camouflage.

We certainly must respect his ability against us but when you put him up against the proper, effective use of the tools God has given us he has nothing. We falter only when we give him the opening. We prevail when we allow God's will to work in our lives.

The Cunning Dragon rightly states that God is his enemy. This is so, not because of Gods wishes, but because of the choice the Cunning Dragon made to follow Lucifer out of God's presence to the Earth. God gives free will to humans and angels alike. We all have the choice to follow God or not.

If you chose something other than God, your enemy has your permission to engage you. Once in, and left unchecked, he will own you. Our strength comes from God, from our relationship with Jesus and from following His word mentally, physically and spiritually.

PREPARATION

No warrior can go into battle effectively unless they are properly prepared. We have many tools and the whole armor of God, as described in Ephesians 6:13-17, is a good place to start. The various pieces of that armor can be brought up as they are called for but remember it is called the *Whole* armor for a reason. Understanding and using it all will protect you in this battle.

As the enemy speaks to his battalion in his opening chapter he talks of us as the target and explains some of the areas he wants his troops to exploit. The first part of the armor that God gives to us through Paul is *"Stand therefore, having girded your waist with truth…"* To the people of Paul's day this image of girding would bring to mind tucking in and fastening the loose clothing that they wore so that it was out of their way and allowed them unencumbered movement. It was a critical first step before battle; preparing for action.

In order to be useful and effective in this battle we must do the basic preparations. We have to be aware that a battle is ongoing and we must know what the opposition looks for to achieve the upper hand.

First we have to believe that the Bible is literal. The Bible is our truth. Jesus is the Word of God and he states "I am the way the *truth* and the life…" (John 14:6) (Italics mine.) When Jesus talks of Satan He is not speaking allegorically as he does with parables. He is speaking of an actual entity with a personality, volition and an agenda. That agenda is made clear in the first part of this manual and is backed up by every piece of scripture that mentions Satan.

We don't deal directly with Satan. He has bigger targets. Knowing how he works, however, tells us how the demons, which we do deal with directly, work. Their motives are the same.

When Satan makes his entrance in the story he starts out with deception. He poses the question to Eve in a way to get her perspective. He may or may not know what God actually said to Adam about the fruit but he asks the question of Eve to see how she responds. This gives him her interpretation of the warning and an idea on how to lay his trap. He asks, *"Has God indeed said, 'you shall not eat of every tree of the garden'?"* Eve's response gives Satan what he needs to continue. *"We may eat the fruit of the trees of the garden; but of the fruit of the tree that is in the midst of the garden, God has said, 'You shall not eat it, nor shall you touch it, lest you die'."* Notice she added to God's direction the part about not touching it. (Gen 2:16-17)

Satan now knows much about his target. She has followed the rule so far, she has added falsely to it, and she is willing to engage Satan and hear what he has to say. He then appeals to her human nature. To paraphrase Gen 3:4-5, he says, "C'mon do you really believe that? If all the rest of this fruit is tasty and beautiful why would he keep you from that tree? You won't die eating the fruit of that tree anymore than you would from eating from the tree next to it. He's keeping something from you! He knows that if you eat it you will be like him and he's trying to keep you in the dark. Do what you want but you're missing out. You could be like God..."

"So when the woman saw that the tree was good for food, that it was pleasant to the eyes, and a tree desirable to make one wise, she took of its fruit and ate. She also gave to her husband with her, and he ate." (Gen 3: 6)

This is where our struggle began, the fall of mankind. Our only defense comes from Jesus. The goal of Christ coming to earth is to overcome the fall and to restore us and the earth to the conditions of the garden. Satan had an awareness of this plan and that is why he tempted Jesus in the wilderness.

Observing Satan as he goes after Jesus reveals that his tactics are consistent. First he waits for a weakness to exploit. The encounter as written in the book of Luke happens after 40 days of fasting. (Luke 4:1-13) Though it speaks of a continual tempting he applies the real pressure when Jesus is weak and hungry. Satan's first request is an appeal to pride and the physical weakness caused by hunger. He starts out subtly questioning Jesus' authority, *"If you are the Son of God..."* Notice the *If*. This sort of challenge is one most of us will rise up to meet. "What do you mean if? I'll show you." Second he gives him a small task. Just turn this stone into bread. Your hungry and surely if would be permissible to get yourself fed.

Jesus doesn't rise to the temptation. He quotes scripture in defense. At this point all Satan needs to win is for Jesus to take any one of his challenges, no matter how small, to have made the perfect lamb imperfect. He doesn't need anything huge just a little compromise will signal victory. Jesus shows us how to defend against this attack. Don't even engage in the temptation. Simply remind yourself and the enemy who it is you serve and what He wants us to do. Focus on God not on Satan during this battle.

His next attack attempts to use pride and maybe to exploit fear. Satan offers to give Jesus authority over all the kingdoms present and future if he will simply worship him. Jesus came to the Earth to re-establish God's kingdom. All authority over all kingdoms past, present and future will be granted to Him by the Father. So Satan is offering a short cut and in the mix is a way out of the pain and suffering to come. Satan is saying I can give you what you came for now and without the crucifixion. Even if Satan is not yet aware of the crucifixion Jesus most likely is. For you and I this would be an easy thing to accept. Jesus again shows us how to deal with this temptation. He sends Satan away and defends his stand with more of God's word.

In the final attempt Satan, seeing the stand of Jesus, attempts to use scripture to apply his points. There are two important things to remember. Satan will adapt to our defenses and he knows more about us, our God and God's word than we ever will in our lifetime. He will use our own weaknesses against us and he will use our strengths, such as the Bible, to work against us as well. Anytime he can use the word of God, either as it is written like he does with Jesus or out of context as he did with Eve, he will use this tool against us.

We cannot defeat him alone. His next technique with Jesus is a testament to that. He can see he is not going to win this time and he leaves. He has no authority to stand up to the commands of Christ. He doesn't give up though. He slinks off to wait for "an opportune time" (Luke 4:13) He plans on coming back.

Our spiritual adversaries use these same techniques with us to push us off the path to the narrow gate; the path Christ invites us to follow. The tactics used by our enemy are used over and over and upon all who live on this earth. *1Cor 10:13 says "No temptation has overtaken you except such as is common to man…"* We can see these tactics at work everywhere we go and we are each tempted regularly. The rest of that passage promises that God *"will not allow you to be tempted beyond what you are able, but with the temptation will also make the way of escape, that you may be able to bear it."* Overcoming the temptation is not automatic even though we are provided a way out. We still have to make the choice.

One aspect of our strength is simply to choose God. Satan only has access to us as we allow it. He is a powerful tempter, but we have all authority to say no to him. When the seventy disciples returned from their first missionary assignment, they were amazed that even the demons where subject to them in Jesus' name. Jesus' response to the disciples, and by default to all who properly follow Jesus, was,

"Behold, I give you authority to tramp on serpents and scorpions, and over all the power of the enemy, and nothing by any means shall hurt you." (Luke 10:19)

In order to have a positive effect in this battle we must rely on the authority of Christ. Our armor is fully effective only if we invite God into our circumstances. The early disciples had Jesus with them physically. We gain this access through regular and effective prayer.

PRAYER

In the 5th chapter of his epistle, James promises that, *"The effective, fervent prayer of a righteous man avails much." (James 5:16).* Fervency is critical. We must have faith that our prayers will be heard and we must be deliberate with our requests. The time spent praying is less important than the focus. When Peter wanted to meet Jesus on the water he stepped out in faith and was able to walk on water. When he took his eyes off of Jesus and began to sink he blurted out "Lord, save me", and Jesus answered the prayer (Matthew 14:30). But if you lay down to sleep, curl up and pray "Lord, be with me and bless everyone" just to check the prayer off of your list you shouldn't expect much of a result.

The fervency James calls for is a great intensity or strong feeling for the desired outcome. Theatrics aren't required but passion is. What you are looking for is complete communication. Simply pray until you are done, without "vain repetition", (Matthew 6:7) no matter how long it takes.

The other piece to insure our prayers avail much is for them to be effective. The key to effective prayer is offered in John,

"If you abide in Me, and My words abide in you, you will ask what you desire,

and it will be done for you." (John 15:7)

The ultimate effective prayer is one that has us seeking God's will for us and not just our perceived needs. Used in this way prayer is a powerful tool that can be used for many reasons: intersession, direction, revelation, forgiveness and protection. Refined, it is a tool to use along with our armor to advance the kingdom of God in this world.

To advance that kingdom we are to use God's authority to resist the Devil. That authority is offered through Christ's work on the cross. In Matt 28:18 Jesus states, *"All authority has been given to Me in heaven and on earth."* Then in Luke 10:19 He grants us that authority over the power of the enemy. In John 16:23 He promises, *"Whatever you ask the Father in My name He will give to you."* Prayer, then, is the vehicle we use to call upon His authority.

Praying in Jesus' name is similar to the concept used in diplomatic circles today. When an ambassador goes to a foreign country to represent the United States he speaks in the name of the President. The Diplomat has the President's permission and authority to perform his duties as directed by him. He is not presenting his own personal agenda but the agenda of the President. We use the same principal in proper prayer. We aren't using a magic incantation; we are speaking with the authority given to us because of our relationship with Jesus. He is our Lord and God and we represent him in that way.

To ask for a selfish concern and adding "in Jesus' name" does nothing to advance our cause and the teaching that it will is a ploy of the Cunning Dragon. Our true power and authority lies in seeking the desires of the Father. Pray as you believe you are being led by Christ and always defer to God by acknowledging, *"nevertheless, not as I will but as you will."(Matthew 26:39)*

Because prayer is a tool that works against your enemy expect opposition. It seems that when you need help the most is when you will feel resistance to sitting down to talk with God. You will often feel the whispers that are sent to convince you that you are not equipped to enter into this conversation. Then, as you wait for an answer, questions may arise that cause you to doubt you were ever heard. It is easy to become discouraged when you don't hear, understand or even get an answer to your prayer.

A prime example of the opposition that can go on in the spiritual realm is offered in Daniel 10: 1-13. When Daniel prayed for direction for his people his answer didn't come for 3 weeks. Daniel was certainly a righteous man and he was fasting and abstaining from comfort so we would have to agree that he was praying with fervency. When the angel finally showed up, he told Daniel:

"Do not fear, Daniel, for from the first day that you set your heart to understand,

and to humble yourself before your God, your words were heard;
and I have come because of your words.
But the prince of the kingdom of Persia withstood me twenty-one days…" (Daniel 10:12-13)

Daniel's prayer was heard immediately but the enemy stood in the way of the messenger with his answer. This angel had to enlist help from Michael, an Archangel, in order to break through. The Cunning Dragon speaks to his battalion of the potential conflicts with other angels. This example shows us that it happens and that it can be overcome.

Prayer is also a way to renew ourselves daily and to keep short accounts with God. God promises to renew his mercies daily (Lamentations 3:22-23) and we do well to return the favor by starting each day with a renewed commitment to dedicating our lives to God.

We often do things that are against God's will. If we let those items fester we open up our armor. Prayer builds our strength. Though it is rightly used when we need help it should regularly be used to support our daily efforts as well.

When talking with God use the template Jesus gives the disciples in the gospels (Mathew 6:9-13). In what is known as The Lord's Prayer Jesus gives us an outline of how we should pray

This prayer is offered not so much as an item to be a memorized, but as an example of how to pray. The elements given by Jesus include praise to God, submission to his will, supplication for our needs, forgiveness of our sin, guidance, protection from our enemies, strength in our weaknesses, agreement that we desire to follow Him and submit to his lordship and that we have a desire for His kingdom. When you pray this way you are strengthening the relationship between you and Jesus

In contrast we are warned that our prayers are not to be used to impress others or to gain the acclaim of those around us.

"but you, when you pray, go into your room,
and when you have shut your door,
pray to your Father who is in the secret place…"
 (Matthew 6:6).

This passage doesn't exclude us from public prayer but it leads us to pray with humility and real purpose. It was an admonishment against the hypocrites who prayed in public for recognition instead of appealing for direction from God.

Prayer is often misunderstood and if it is then its power is diluted. It should not be uncomfortable. It is simply talking with, and listening to, God. But prayer is not a device to force God to change his will. It is a tool for us to be conformed to Him so that we follow His will. In our context it is used to buoy up our defensive and offensive positions while we are working for God's Kingdom.

RIGHTEOUSNESS

We have the ability to stand before God in prayer due to the righteousness granted to us by Christ's work on the cross. We acquire this righteousness through our prayers to give ourselves over to Christ.

To be righteous is to have a right standing with God. The Bible shows us over and over again that we have not been able to do that in our own might. Therefore we have the righteousness of Christ imputed, or credited, to us. Jesus did His work on the cross to both impute His righteousness to us and to have our sins imputed to Him. (In the case of our sins being imputed to Christ it means He has taken the blame for all of our sinful actions past, present and future.) In this trade we get all of the benefit and Jesus takes on all of the blame. Because of this imputation we stand before our Father with the same ease that Jesus stands before Him.

This is a powerful offering that the Cunning Dragon uses continually to wear us down. He knows our tendency to feel the guilt and to express our unworthy nature. He is using the truth to spin the offer so we will not embrace it. Alone we are not worthy of this gift but it is free for us to accept. Even though we have not earned the gift we are encouraged by our

Lord to accept it and to enter in to the romance He wants us to experience.

In this battle the breastplate protects the warrior's heart. The power of our breastplate doesn't come from us but from the righteousness of Jesus. The accuser will try desperately to make you realize that you are not worthy to stand before God. The defense for that is admitting that it is so and boldly accepting that Jesus has protected us from this type of attack. We can stand confidently because of the righteousness of Christ.

All that we are, when we are acting on God's behalf, is due to the work of Jesus on the cross. We will still feel the struggles of this world but a huge burden is lifted when we accept that we walk protected by Christ.

The Christmas song "Good King Wenceslas" is an example of how this works. The King and his page are setting out to help a poor, hungry man on a cold, winter night. They set out to bring him food and wine but during the journey to this man's home the page grows tired and can't continue on his own. Toward the end of the song come the words that inspire us in our struggle as we follow Jesus:

Page and monarch forth they went
Forth they went together
Through the rude wind's wild lament
And the bitter weather

"Sire, the night is darker now
And the wind blows stronger
Fails my heart, I know not how,
I can go no longer."
"Mark my footsteps, my good page
Tread thou in them boldly
Thou shalt find the winter's rage
Freeze thy blood less coldly."

In his master's steps he trod
Where the snow lay dinted
Heat was in the very sod
Which the Saint had printed.

We are the page and Christ is the monarch. With confidence and humility we should follow Jesus in our lives. As we travel, we should rely on the protection of Jesus. If we walk in his footsteps, he makes the path ready for us. We still have to move ahead but the footprints of Christ make the path clearer and easier. Our enemy may be able to point out a less difficult path for us to follow but that path leads to our destruction. We can choose to follow on a path that leads to life, even with its struggles, or coast easily on the other.

The things of this world offer us little apart from our acceptance of Christ's promise and our enemy would have us rely on our own work and deny

Christ's part in our life. Paul offers an example of how we should approach this situation,

"...not having my own righteousness, which is from the law, but that which is through faith in Christ, the righteousness which is from God by faith;" (Philippians 3:9)

Properly used, the breastplate of righteousness is an impenetrable defense for our heart. When we fully accept the promise of Christ and allow His righteousness into our lives, we are fully protected. We will slip in our daily attempts so we must return by using prayer to keep short accounts and renew ourselves daily to our God and to this romance.

OUR STRENGTH AND OUR WEAKNESS

This entire world, all of its kingdoms, all that we see here has been given to Satan by the fall of Adam. As imperfect humans we also grant authority over ourselves to our enemy through our sin. Jesus, the second Adam, came to win this world back. We only have to accept His gift and join in the fight. If we don't accept Christ we revert to our default position.

There are only two kingdoms: The kingdom of God and light or the kingdom of Satan and darkness. These are the only choices. Certainly one can deliberately choose Satan but to wander around without a conscious decision to choose God automatically places us into the kingdom of darkness. We must actively choose God.

Although we live in a physical and fallen world we are first spiritual beings. The battle is initiated in the spiritual world. It is from there that God calls to us and it is from there that the enemy shoots his fiery darts.

Even though this all starts in the spiritual realm we are tempted through the imperfections of this world and our physical body. In our unperfected form we are vulnerable to many stresses and longings. So much so that our enemy only has to dabble in the physical to lure us away.

Satan will always capitalize on the perceived similarities between God and himself in an attempt to lead you to believe they are equal. Though Satan is certainly opposite of God he is not equal. He is pure evil and he has limitations. Once he is aware of you knowing that, he will move to build up your confidence that you can battle him without help. Never fall into the lie that we are capable of going toe to toe with him. We must always call on the authority of Christ and the power he gives us in order to win.

As stated by The Cunning Dragon, these enemies want to topple us in our strengths by exploiting our weaknesses. We must renew and refresh ourselves daily in order to remain strong. Not every day will pose a struggle. When the enemy performs a tactical retreat it becomes easy for us to forgo our daily prayer time because everything is going well. Several days of that will make us weak. That is when the attack is likely to recur. If it is strong enough we may just give in to the temptation of the negative emotion it causes and listen to the whispers that God doesn't really care.

The enemy's goal is to distract us from calling on God for help. In that scenario we lose and for many this has caused a downward spiral that becomes harder to overcome with each passing day. This is one of the ways the enemy lures us into the covenants written of by The Cunning Dragon.

These are the covenants we make with our adversary, or ourselves, which hold a door open to them. A common covenant mentioned by The Cunning Dragon is a cursory acknowledgment that Christ died for the sins of the believer but that your sins are somehow not included in that promise. If you make this covenant you are, in essence, calling God a liar. Once that opening is established the enemy will continually use it as a way to wear you down.

When God has offered His grace to forgive us of our sin who are we to minimize that? Consider his word,

"As far as the east is from the west, so far has He removed our transgressions from us." (Psalms 103:12).

If you start at the equator and travel north toward the pole you are going north until you reach the pole. In the next step you are going south. It is the same if you start out by heading south. When you reach the South Pole your next step is to the north. Now start at the equator and walk along it to the east. When do you begin heading west on this course? Never. That is the image given by God.

The separation of our sins from Him is a gap that is unreachable. He truly doesn't choose to recall or consider any sin from which you have confessed and repented. If you allow your remorse or guilt to carry on in your life you have made a covenant with that remorse or guilt and the enemy has a permissible place to enter into a conversation with you. Cancel that covenant. Rescind that promise and close that opening in your armor.

If you are a born-again Christian the Holy Spirit dwells in your heart. Because of that a demon can't be there too. Their access is external, but they can certainly use that access to affect us physically and emotionally. If you start to feel an emotion that doesn't fit either your personality or the actual events of the moment, consider that you may be under spiritual attack and engage the authority of Christ to defeat the attack.

ASSURING YOUR SPOT ON THE CONTINUUM

The Cunning Dragon gives his list of targets by way of his Continuum. He states that all are his target, but the focus is on those who have a relationship with Jesus.

The typical readers of this book either are truly Christian or have no reason to believe that they are not. We must first sort through the distortions that have been implemented by our enemy and define Biblical Christianity.

Merrian-Webster.com states that a Christian is: One who professes belief in the teachings of Jesus Christ. Answers.com states: One who professes a belief in Jesus as Christ or follows the religion based on the life and teachings of Jesus. One who lives according to the teachings of Jesus.

These definitions are true of a Christian but they are not complete. One can profess a belief in Christ without choosing to follow Him and one can believe incorrectly. *Even the demons believe --and tremble! (James 2:19).* Just believing that Jesus exists doesn't make one a Christian.

Following a religion based on the teachings of Jesus or living according to those teachings can easily put you in the category described by the Cunning Dragon as "Followers of Our Way". If you are truly a Christian by Christ's definition these examples will describe you but we need to delve deeper for a security in our faith.

The Apostle Paul states in Philippians 3:3 that we as Christians *"… worship God in the spirit, rejoice in Christ Jesus, and have no confidence in the flesh."* That last part is a critical defining point. The reason for concern is because we often rely on religion, our man-made processes, to reach God and to define our Christianity. Christ desires a relationship with us based on His criteria. These criteria are simple in their presentation but can be made difficult by our human nature.

Biblically the most basic, yet complete description of a Christian is one who follows Romans 10:8-10:

"The word is near you, in your mouth and in your heart" (That is the word of faith which we preach): that if you confess with your mouth the Lord Jesus and believe in your heart that God has raised Him from the dead, you will be saved."

This is truly simple but you can see how the other definitions fail if this part is not in place.

The Cunning Dragon, and his ilk, has worked since the beginning to convince us that we have to do something to enhance this process. He urges us to trust that we can't just speak it and believe it, we must do good works and make altars and create ceremony and worship a physical emblem before things can be right with God. Why would this be a tactic? Because what Christ asks of us is so simple the enemy must look for ways to discourage us by complicating it. To make matters worse we often can't believe in the simplicity of the process.

Let me make a distinction, the process is simple but for many not easy. (Simple= not complicated, easy= not difficult) The steps we need to take to accept Christ are not complicated but they can be difficult.

I remember a friend urging me to become a Christian. He said, "Just accept Christ!" this was a process that he found so simple he could not comprehend my reluctance. My response was that I could say to him that I had accepted Christ but if this God were really omniscient, He would know I was lying. I had, in my opinion, to first come to an informed determination that the things my friend told me about Jesus were true. What he asked of me was simple once I overcame the difficulty of acquiring the intellectual proof my logical mind required.

If the enemy can convince us that more is required he has a better chance of discouraging us. Don't overthink the question. Examine God's word but don't assume more than what is there.

For instance, "Remember the Sabbath day and keep it holy." The fourth commandment in its basic content refers to taking a day off during the week. This includes you, all in your household and your beasts of burden. Simple, but through religion and our attempt to add our individual interpretation it is not easy for some. Following the text it is simply stating that God rested on the 7th day and so should you. This is the time unfettered by other distractions that you are to focus in on the restorative relationship with Jesus. It is a time to rest in the arms of a loving God.

One can go to the various lists of the attachments to this law from various sects and see that people have added hundreds of restrictions to how this commandment is to be fulfilled. Why must it be difficult? For the most part it is our belief that we must be doing something, or sacrificing something, in order for this law to be acceptable by God. Whether this is brought on by human pride or the whisperings of the enemy it draws us away from the simplicity of God. Yes, there are rules, but He really only wants us to join Him in a romance.

Let's return to Paul's directive. Following it will allow the rest to fall into place. You can be generally defined by those dictionary definitions but the full manifestation of a relationship with Jesus is exhibited by these things:

*Repentance. It is made apparent by the commands of Christ and the Apostles that this is a requirement. (Luke 13:3, Acts 3:19). If you desire a relationship with Jesus you will crave a true repentance. Believing that Jesus is your God you will have the desire to serve Him. This shows itself as a passion to be right before God.

*From there the Holy Spirit indwells you and your body becomes His temple, (1Corinthians 6:19).

*You are born again, previously of the flesh but now of the Spirit (John 3:3-7)

*Then, though you have to nurture the new relationship, you are a child of God and are written in the Lamb's book of life (Revelation 21:27, Luke 10:20).

Anything that we try to add to this basic process has the ability to dilute its power. Our enemy works diligently to convince us to confuse and compound the difficulty of following our path. What makes the "difficult path" difficult is our human desire to be in control and to add items to the list. The Cunning Dragon will play on this desire by offering suggestions to encourage it through his whispers.

Being Christian we certainly have other duties and commands to follow. All of them show an outward sign to others of our salvation, but none of them are a requirement of Salvation. When you are established in Christ you will be inclined to do good things for the kingdom and you will want to follow the commands of baptism and communion as an act of love and remembrance. This is good and desired as long as the focus is on Jesus and not on the ceremony.

The outward signs of one who has done the two step process above (confess and believe) is revealed in the following statement of faith as described by more than a few Bible teaching churches.

**The 66 books of the Old and New Testament are, in their original form, the infallible word of God.

**There is only one God. He is eternal, omnipotent and perfect. He is one God consisting of three distinct persons. These three are God the Father, God the Son and God the Holy Spirit.

**All humans are corrupt by nature because of the original sin that occurred in the Garden. This separates us from God.

**We are saved by Grace alone through faith alone by the work of Jesus upon the cross. Jesus, the second person of the Godhead, condescended to Earth as a man to live a perfect life and die the sacrificial death on the cross to redeem us of our sins.

**Those who, by faith, receive this free gift of atonement will live forever in the fellowship of the one and true living God.

**The true Christian church is made up of all people who have this saving faith in Jesus Christ and have been regenerated by the work of the Holy Spirit, who is the third person of the Godhead.

As we consider this in the spirit of intellect, we have to be certain that we are not swayed by emotion. The points above must be in place in order for you to be a saved, born again Christian. No matter what else you do for the Kingdom of God, without these things you fall into the enemy's grasp. Without the previous items in place none of the following things in and of themselves will save you: going to church, being a member of a particular denomination or organization, having been baptized, believing Jesus was only a man who existed in our history as a good teacher or prophet, or any amount of good deeds. The salvation Christ speaks of is brought to us by His grace alone through your faith alone. (Romans 11:6, Ephesians 2:5, 2:9 etc.)

There is debate, as well, on who among us can be saved by the above criteria. The simple, but not simplistic, answer is everyone who chooses to be. See: John 3:15, 6:40, 6:47 Mark 9:23, Acts 10:43 Romans 1:16 1John 5:1

We must first be called by God, (John 6:44, Romans 8:28-30), but he makes that call to everyone.

"The Lord is not slack concerning His promise, as some count slackness, but is longsuffering toward us, not willing that any should perish but that all would come to repentance." (2Peter 3:9)

In each of these passages the terms are definitive. God calls "All" and accepts "Any" and "Every". The deciding factor here is what free willed people choose to do with this information.

All can be saved but not all will be. This is the premise of the attack by the Cunning Dragon. He relishes the fact that even Jesus admits that "Few will find it" as it pertains to the narrow gate. But knowing this is the focus of an attack our responsibility is to be aware of the tactic and to deflect it from ourselves and others as we see it happen to them. We can't call anyone to Christ. That is only done through the Holy Spirit. But we can tell people what we believe with gentleness and respect.

"But sanctify the Lord God in your hearts, and always be ready to give a defense to everyone who asks you a reason for the hope that is in you, with meekness and fear." (1 Peter 3:15)

THE ROMANCE

There is a song by the late Christian musician, Keith Green, entitled "Asleep In the Light" that sums up much of what we should do and what we actually do as a global group. One line in particular describes our current state.

"The world is sleeping in the dark,
That the church just can't fight, cause it's asleep in the light" (*Sparrow Records*)

This slumber of the church and its followers is at the heart of this warfare. Those who are "asleep in the light" either ignore or avoid the possibility of a spiritual attack. Loss of passion for the romance is the toll of our defeat. How can we fully appreciate the grandeur of the romance without acknowledging the severity of the battle?

Imagine you are romantically involved with someone who loves you dearly. And you love them. You then meet with another for a tryst in their bed. Your beloved finds out and you say you will never do it again so they forgive you. This forgiveness is so complete that in their eyes it not only is it forgotten but it is as if it never happened. With that forgiveness you go out and repeat your transgression. You again confess and again are forgiven. Then you do it again. This time you want to return but your new lover refuses to let you go. Now your beloved battles for you to the point of death to be sure you are set free because that is their only desire. You are so important that they will find a way to release you no matter the cost to them. While watching your beloved's struggle to get you out of the house of the new lover you vacillate between wanting to stay and wanting to be set free. Even seeing your vacillation your beloved loves you so desperately that they continue to do battle for your freedom. And even as you waiver between your options your Beloved dies to secure your freedom. His only request is that you accept what he did for you and chose Him in the end. This is the story told in the Bible about Christ and His church.

We cannot move ahead with only a passing flirtation with Christ. We must love Him, live his commandments, tell others of Him and be hopelessly lost in this romance. If He will do that much for us we can do no less for Him.

The question often asked is if Christ loves us so much how could there be any chance that someone will not be with him in the end? The answer is in the gift and the burden of our free will. We have to be informed and then make a deliberate choice to follow Jesus.

The enemy will do whatever he can to hide from us or repel us from the narrow gate. He will even use the scripture's promise that the path is difficult. How can we justify the concept of the difficult path to a narrow gate? Why would a loving God make this so hard? Remember the distinction between simple and easy. Accepting Christ is simple, what we bring to the table is what makes it hard. Without protecting our thoughts the enemy will have access to offer whispers that discourage us.

The standard argument for skeptics is if there is a loving God how can He… allow suffering, let children die, cause this struggle in my life, etc, etc (you fill in the blanks). For our topic the blank is "only allow a narrow gate that He knows few will find?" All of the blanks listed have the same basic answer. God has given us the dignity of a free will. If what He wants from us is a romance then he must not force the love coming from us. So He makes the offer and allows us to choose.

Simple but not easy.

The trouble with having a choice is we tend to lay blame elsewhere for the outcome of what we have chosen. The fact that the choices of those around us can affect our lives is part and parcel of our fallen world and the spiritual warfare that surrounds us. We may use our free will in an attempt to do good while others around us use their free will to hinder us. We have to contend with this fallen world while we attempt to make the right choices. If we want to do what is right but the things going on around us tend to push against that choice we tend to blame God. From our standpoint His allowing this struggle could easily be considered unfair and unloving. He is a God of justice. Why would He allow this strife?

To understand God's justice we must pull ourselves out of the context of our world. The impurity of where we live will tarnish the definitions and expected outcome of our thought process. Justice is merited reward or punishment through the administration of the law.

If justice is the merited reward or punishment by God's law we deserve no reward from what we do here apart from Jesus. The Bible makes that clear *"there is none righteous no not one." (Romans 3:10 referring to Psalms 14:1-3)*

All sins are equal in two ways. Any sin, no matter how small, separates us from God. (Romans 6:13)

And all sins, no matter how heinous, can be forgiven by God.

It is fair to say in our daily dealings we often lean toward mercy. It makes sense that we would because God is so gracious in this category and we are made in his image. But when this story comes to a close true justice is the required move by God. True justice dictates that anyone who has any wrong doing in any part of their life must be judged. If any sin is uncovered the one with that sin must suffer the merited consequence. By our ideals of mercy this seems grossly unfair.

The narrow gate is our salvation from this outcome. Accepting Christ and following the mandates of a true Christian, without relying on our religious additions, covers our sin with the righteousness of Christ and allows us to enter the father's presence as if we were now, and had always been, sin free.

According to God's word few will choose that. Is that fair? I say certainly, based on our merit. There is no perfect example in a secular sense but I think of the attitude I have seen grow quite prevalent lately in school and church sporting events. "You are all winners" is a common cry and in order to facilitate that premise we can play a sport but we won't keep score. Or we will play but if you get a certain amount ahead your scores will no longer count until the other team catches up. My competitive nature, given to me by God, says this isn't right; it isn't just. If you look at it from the lower scoring teams side a parent may believe that it is best for their child's self esteem. If you look at it from the higher scorer's side you get the feeling that it doesn't pay to sweat and work if there is no reward at the end. Justice requires that merit on both sides be addressed. If I merit a win I should enjoy the reward. If I merit a loss I must endure the consequences.

And that is the point. Would it be fair for us to follow the rules laid out by God, give up some of the things others in this world seek to enjoy, place our trust in Christ and be dedicated to the cause, only to find out that our secular neighbor, our unrepentant adulterous congressman, Hitler or even Satan, ends up with the same reward as we do? Where is the justice in that? How could a loving God allow *that* to happen?

Justice cannot allow it. So no matter how much I want everyone to reap the benefit of the promise, I have to admit that without making the required choice, no matter how wonderful they are otherwise, they can not, by the nature of our God, be allowed the promised reward.

Emotionally this may be an extreme challenge but logically it falls into place.

I believe in God's eyes it is also completely fair. Not just because He wants it to be (as we might factor something) but also because it can be factored logically within the parameters we work with in understanding God.

Intellectual Defense

The protection offered by the armor of God for any intellectual attack is the Helmet of Salvation and the enemy wants to be sure this item is ineffective. In a physical battle the helmet protects the head; in this spiritual battle it protects the thoughts that drive our actions. Though it is used to protect our thoughts and what comes into our head, it is not to limit us in our thinking. The enemy will try to confuse what salvation is and how it is achieved. It is certainly in his interest to make it seem obscure, unfair and difficult at best to secure. We must focus on how the promise of salvation protects our thoughts.

We are born into a fallen world already at a disadvantage. God calls us but without taking the step to accept His offer we are destined for the abyss. There is nothing we can do for ourselves to garner favor with God. Knowing this God condescends to our world; sets aside his devine nature, becomes a human and goes through all of the struggles we face without falling into sin. This sets Him up to be the perfect sacrifice for mankind. He then chooses to die for us. He takes on all our collective sin, is for a time separated from the Father and then allows men to kill him. He rises on the third day and later ascends back to the right hand of the Father. This is all done so that we, who cannot save ourselves, may put on the righteousness of Christ so that we can commune with the Father.

If that story of Christ described as it is in scripture doesn't inspire you, you may not fully understand its implication. When fully understood it should cause everything you think and do to be prefaced by what has been done for you. Every thought should be taken captive to Christ. (2 Corinthians 10:5) When you feel fear or doubt or are drawn toward a poor choice think of the sacrifice given for you. When the enemy tempts you rely on the helmet to protect your thoughts. How can we choose to do the wrong thing when so much has been given to allow us to be children of God? These are not platitudes. This is real life and real justice will come from our choices. Our thoughts are protected because of the assurance offered by the gift of salvation.

Salvation comes to us through accepting Christ and His work upon the cross. Nothing else. Understanding this makes it clear why the enemy wants to confuse the definition and promise of Christianity. The enemy's objective is to complicate what is simple and to add difficulty to our understanding or acceptance of this call from Jesus. The protection of our thoughts, our helmet, comes through the intellectual knowledge of what our salvation through Christ provides.

The work of the cross was completed in three steps.

1) Jesus suffered and died for our sins. We are not able to walk sinless in this life so we needed a pure sacrifice, as laid out by the Old Testament law, to atone for these sins.
2) Jesus rose from the dead. This speaks to the fact that we too will rise again in perfection so that we can be fully with God. Without the work of the cross we would be dead in our sins and never have a Father/child relationship with Him
3) Jesus ascended into heaven to be at the right hand of God. He was given all authority in heaven and on earth to overcome the Evil One. This is the key. He grants us that authority to defend ourselves in this battle.

"Behold, I give you the authority to trample on serpents and scorpions,
 and over all the power of the enemy, and nothing shall by any means hurt you." (Luke 10:19)

This authority was given to others beyond the 12 Apostles. We can rest in the fact that just like the early followers of Christ we are included in receiving this authority. (See Mark 16:17 & 13:34) Our enemy is afraid of us taping into this power. He will attempt to make you believe that you are to be a god and trust in yourself instead of relying on Jesus to overcome him. The first, if you believe it, allows him access under your helmet. Relying on Jesus allows us to win this battle both in the physical and spiritual realm.

Faith in Christ must have a spiritual connection; intellectual belief need not be so. The enemy, working in the physical, will try to hinder your faith through your intellect. Faith being *"the substance of things hoped for..."* makes it an easy target for intellectual skepticism. So we must develop a way to make our faith logically based. We are to rely on our faith but it is never required to be blind.

One of the tools of the enemy is to have Christians seem ignorant and illogical to those around them so that doubt might creep in. The intent is to cause Christians to question the veracity of why they believe in Christ. But our God asks us to consider his offer with thought and reason. *"Come now let us reason together" Isa 1:18*. If God gave us the ability to think and reason then we must be able to use these tools to understand, at least as far as we are able as humans, who He is and what He wants from us.

What do these tools tell us about why the gate is narrow and the path difficult? God does not establish it this way. This definition is true based on the fact that His invitation to join the romance largely goes against our sinful, physical nature. We want autonomy. We want freedom. We want independence. Trusting in someone else (Jesus) seems foreign to our nature. We have to make a deliberate choice to seek and follow the path He calls us to. It is difficult because not only are Christians a bit resistant to the path but also those around us in this world are opposed to this message. This is a tool the enemy will use to lead us away. If he can keep us resistant and have others mock and oppose us we can be led to not try so hard to follow this difficult path. We are likely to look for a shortcut. If we fall into this trap the enemy has us cornered.

The Cunning Dragon repeatedly returns to the premise of using our physical world against us. He teaches his followers to divert us from a deeper spiritual knowledge by keeping us occupied with our physical wants, needs and desires.

The focus of what we want and need in the physical world comes from our thoughts. It is our thoughts that lead us to sin, it is our thoughts that lead us to doubt Gods desires, and it is our thoughts that cause us to doubt the simplicity of God and his offer of a romance. If the enemy can infiltrate our mind he has the type of control he desires.

Just as our thoughts without God's protection can lead us away it is also our thoughts, protected by God, that lead us to life. If our thoughts are protected we will think of Christ, salvation, heaven and the positive spiritual aspect of our nature. This is another reason for the path being difficult. We have to apply effort to get to this point.

In Galatians Paul tells the church:

"Do not be deceived, God is not mocked; for whatever a man sows, that he will also reap. For he who sows to his flesh will of the flesh reap corruption, but he who sows to the spirit will of the spirit reap everlasting life." (Galatians 6:7-8)

He goes on to encourage us to not grow weary and not to lose heart. We are in a battle against a strong and cunning enemy. We are not given a pass as we accept Christ. In fact in many ways this turns up the heat against us. Our enemy wants us to be tired and discouraged. If he can't remove us from the book of life he wants to be certain that our lives don't lead others to choose Christ. Expect opposition but always return to the romance. *If God is for us who can be against us? (Romans 8:31)* This doesn't mean we won't have opposition, it means that we can rely on a victory if we trust God.

As you struggle with your issues in this world the Cunning Dragon will try to whisper anything that will help you to move away from the love of Jesus to the utter despair this world has to offer. If he can keep you on a physical course he can pull you away from the relationship that will keep you whole. Our physical distress is real and felt daily; our hope of heaven is real, but we can't touch or see it. When we are worn out it is easy to put that hope on the back burner. Let's look deeply into the helmet of salvation so that we can confidently pull it over our head.

When we give our lives to Christ we are saved. That is a wonderful thing but the passion in many fades quickly. During times of difficulty we often think if I am saved why is my life still so difficult? Consider this: We are saved unto salvation. The promise of our salvation is a future event. We look forward to its fulfillment. We err to believe that the work is complete here and now. When Christ spoke from the cross "it is finished" He spoke of the vehicle for salvation, yet its fulfillment is still in our individual futures.

Don't misunderstand me. If you have given your life to Christ and accepted Him as your Savior, you are certainly saved. You now have a hope as defined in the biblical language. Hope in this respect is a faithful expectation. It is not to be regarded as "I might be saved." It is a definitive "I can count on that salvation." The enemy, though, can work against that faithful belief by harping on the struggles you have in your day-to-day world. Keep in mind the difference. You are saved today. You are promised the fulfillment of that salvation when you are with Christ.

When Jesus asks you to take on his yoke because it is light and his burden is easy, he speaks truthfully but that we have a yoke and a burden means that we still have work to do. We still have toils with which we deal. Doing His work to advance the kingdom should be a part of what drives us. We look forward to the hope of the future life with Christ and the hope of heaven. We still have to live here now, we still must do the work we are called to do and we must still struggle with the temptations and the cares of this world. During it all our assignment, our call, is to advance the kingdom.

"For Godly sorrow produces repentance leading to salvation, not to be regretted; but the sorrow of the world produces death." (2Corinthians 7:10)

This passage refers to the difference of a true sorrow for the transgression against God vs. the sorrow of getting caught in a transgression that you would have no sorrow for otherwise. Because we sin daily this points to the fact that we must continually work toward the day of the fulfillment of our salvation. Philippians 2:12 also speaks of a continual process. :"*…work out your own salvation with fear and trembling."*

If we are diligent to follow that command God will certainly keep his promise to us.

"Blessed be the God and Father of our Lord Jesus Christ, who according to His abundant mercy has begotten us again to a living hope through the resurrection of Jesus Christ from the dead, to an inheritance incorruptible and undefiled and that does not fade away, reserved in heaven for you, who are kept by the power of God through faith for salvation ready to be revealed in the last time." (1Peter 1:3-5)

This passage is rich with promise. The "living hope" is what we enjoy now. The promise of the future of our salvation is perfection yet to come. This inheritance is permanent and unchanging. And it is reserved in heaven for you. So we are guaranteed this reward but we are still to work our way through this world before it is fulfilled. The key is to not allow these struggles to become a foothold for the enemy. You will find discouragement and will feel pulled down by these struggles but if you turn to God for comfort the Holy Spirit will heal your discouragement. Wait for Him with expectation.

You must be prepared when you put your back to the yoke of Jesus. Your enemy will not just stand by and watch. The more you work and the more effective you become the more hated you will be. Your enemy will do what he can to make your life hard. The goal is to get you to say to yourself, "Maybe my life will be easier if I just accept my salvation quietly. That should keep me off the enemy's radar." It won't keep you off the radar but it will certainly be marked as a victory for Satan. And offer up another chink in your armor.

OUR CALLING

The Apostle Paul said "...*to live is Christ and to die is gain.*" He goes on in that chapter to say that to die would be a better prospect for him but that his staying and doing the work he was called to do would be better for those he could reach while he was here. (See Philippians 1:21-26). We are to follow this example. It is harder to put ourselves into the fight then to not, but it so much more rewarding. And it is what Jesus calls us to do.

Many places in the bible speak of spreading the gospel. It is to be our purpose in this physical world. Your enemy will always oppose this, both spiritually and physically. The hope of heaven gives us the boldness to push ahead without fear. I can understand fearing the mechanism of our death but we ought to be able to embrace the concept of "to die is gain." We should never seek our own death but if you are not ready to die then you cannot fully live.

One of the ways the enemy gets a foothold is through the struggles we have in this life. It is hard to overcome the fear and anger of a definitive crisis now by saying "well, all will be fixed in the next life". You still have to live with the joys and struggles of this world.

The enemy does well to have you dwell on the current hardships at the expense of the future glory.

And let's face it, when wallowing in the current mire the future glory is hard to focus upon. Yet, it is there as certainly as anything you can see or grasp before you. Our defense throughout this battle is the intellectual and heartfelt confidence we have in the promise of the salvation offered by Christ. Truly believing and accepting that gift is all we need.

"You believe that there is one God. You do well. Even the demons believe—and tremble!" (James 2:19)

This verse in James taken in its full context speaks of the evident fruit of one who has a true saving faith. We must have the fruit of our salvation written into our lives. If the enemy can convince you that being baptized in a particular church is the way to salvation and that is what you do to feel saved it doesn't matter how much more you do for the kingdom, you have fallen into the enemy's trap. You can say you believe in Jesus and his work upon the cross, you may even believe you are saved by whatever it is that you do with your belief, but *"faith without works is dead". (James 2:20)*.

The Cunning Dragon makes it clear to his minion that not everyone has achieved salvation. They have perfected the techniques designed to lead a seeker to the point of belief in salvation without taking the simple steps Christ asks of us. Without those steps there is no salvation. The Bible makes it clear that all can be saved and there is only one way to achieve that salvation. Jesus is that way.

"Nor is there salvation in any other, for there is no other name under heaven given among men by which we must be saved."
(*Acts 4:12*) (Speaking of Jesus)

" 'I am the way, the truth and the life. No one comes to the Father except through Me.' " (*John 14:6*) (Jesus speaking.)

"...that if you confess with your mouth the Lord Jesus and believe in your heart that God raised Him from the dead, you will be saved." (*Romans 10:9*)

"For God so loved the world that he gave his only begotten Son, that whoever believes in Him should not perish but have everlasting life. For God did not send His Son into the world to condemn the world, but that the world through Him might be saved."
(*John 3:16-17*)

These passages all testify to the fact that the choice to be saved is an individual one. All people have the option but *"...there are few who will find it."* Scriptures also speak of more than just an intellectual belief. Issues of faith and the heart must be included. We have to come to knowledge and faith that Christ can and will save us if we just accept his free gift of grace and salvation. This is a fine example of how all the pieces of our armor must be used in harmony.

CONDITIONS OF SALVATION

There are many points of duty to our faith that we can respectfully debate but nothing else can be added to this list that is a requirement of salvation. In fact we are commanded by Jesus to do several things. If we are able we should do those things willingly. They are not, however, elements of Salvation.

This is where the Cunning Dragon leads his battalion to focus. If we, as believers in Christ, forget or forego a required element of salvation for something else that is commanded but not required we can be drawn away from God.

He asks you to be baptized as an outward sign of your inward commitment. The inward is what saves you the outward is its symbol. Must you be baptized? It is certainly a directive of Jesus but if it is a requirement of Salvation Jesus lied to the thief on the cross when He said, *"Assuredly, I say to you, today you will be with me in Paradise" (Luke 23:43)*. There was no opportunity for a baptism yet he was assured his place in heaven. The salvation of the thief was guaranteed by his faith in Christ. This example wasn't offered to us as an exception. Our salvation is guaranteed in the same way.

The command to partake in communion is given to us to remind us of all that Christ did for us on the cross. That He would take our place so we could have that romance with God is a gift beyond description. To ceremonially partake in communion should be considered an honor, but nowhere does the bible lead us to believe it is a requirement of salvation.

Must you do good works? According to the Book of James these works are the outpouring of the Spirit not a requirement of salvation. The enemy uses this one often. If you do more good than bad everything is fine. The following text about faith and works is used to teach both perspectives.

" What does it profit, my brethren, if someone says he has faith but does not have works? Can faith save him? If a brother or a sister is naked and destitute of daily food, and one of you says to them, "Depart in peace, be warmed and filled," but you do not give them the things which are needed for the body, what does it profit? Thus also faith by itself, if it does not have works, is dead.' "
(James 2:14-18)

"Can faith save him?" is a line that is often distorted. James' whole argument is that you may say you have saving faith but if your life doesn't change do you really? A natural outcome of the Holy Spirit living in you is a compulsion to do good works. The argument must be taken in context of the bigger picture. Ephesians 2:8-9 backs this up by showing that faith and not works is what saves you. Otherwise our pride will puff up and we will believe our salvation has been done by something we have accomplished and not by God's gift.

We need not follow dietary laws, Sabbath laws, temple laws or the like. Jesus stated that he did not come to abolish those laws but to fulfill them. There may be no harm in following them but your salvation does not depend on them.

Anything that will cause us to doubt our relationship with God will be a tool our enemy uses to achieve his goal. To guard against this we have to strengthen our knowledge and understanding of what salvation really means to us and what it looks like in our physical world. The process of salvation on our part is simple. Don't complicate it only fully accept it. In this way you will more easily overcome the devices of our enemy.

OVERCOMING THE DEVICES OF OUR ENEMY

A device, as used by The Cunning Dragon, is a scheme or trick intended to deceive. The tools and devices available for his use are many and varied. They have the ability to overlap each other and to be adapted to our response. If we focus on all that can be used against us we will become overwhelmed. To simplify our offensive and defensive position we must focus on Jesus as our protector. He already knows what is in store for us and is open about it.

"In the world you will have tribulation; but be of good cheer, I have overcome the world." (John 16:33)

He is promising us that even though our struggles are inevitable He is with us and will lead us to victory if we allow it. Looking at this battle in perspective we will have an easier time of it if we allow Christ to lead us and to fall under His covering. He has overcome the world and we, by proxy, have this ability as well.

No matter what tool or device our enemy uses against us our advocate is the only tool we need to defend our stand. We don't need to come up with new and varied options to try to deflect all of the tactics of the enemy. All of their attacks are held at bay by our one tool our faith in Christ and His work upon the cross.

The Bible declares that God is our protection in so many ways. He is our: defense, deliverer, fortress, hiding place, high tower, refuge, rock, salvation, strength and power, strong habitation and dwelling place. When going into battle, any warrior would welcome any one of these items. If we dwell with God we have them all. If we get out of His way we have no reason to fear the enemy. Our strength in Christ is complete. Our weakness comes only from within because we rely too often on a personal defense.

The enemy's intent is to penetrate any portion of our armor that he can get behind. His objective is to do damage from within. In order to defend against this type of attack our mode of defense has to be versatile. This defines the Shield of Faith, which is the tool we are to use to protect us from the weakness provided by our flesh.

In battle the shield is a movable piece of armor that protects all of the body including that which is covered by the permanent armor. The Shield of Faith must never be laid down and must be directed at times as double coverage over the other pieces of armor as those areas are being targeted.

In the early days of our conversion we have an undeveloped faith. At that stage it is often our enthusiasm that makes things work. This undeveloped faith can be likened to a buckler which is a small shield worn on the arm. This is a time when we feel the most pressure to reconsider our belief. The parable of the sower is in play at this stage. (Matthew 13:3-9) This is the first opportunity, as a Christian, that the enemy has a chance to pull us back into the world and it is when we are usually the most vulnerable. Since we are working with a smaller shield we will have to work constantly to deflect the flaming darts. As we grow in the knowledge of Christ the shield enlarges and offers us better protection. When we work side by side with other believers our combined shields become a true wall that offers us our best protection. The only way for it to be penetrated by the enemy is if we lower it or set it aside. We must always be strengthening that shield. We have to be relying on a faith that is developed by intellect in order for it to be effective.

In Biblical context faith is a solid belief in an outcome.

"Now faith is the substance of things hoped for, the evidence of things not seen." (Ephesians 11:1)

The key words in this passage for the warrior are "substance" and "evidence". (Not "hoped for" and "unseen" as some define them). We tend to look at hope as a desire; something we *want* to happen, not something that we fully *expect* to happen. Blind faith depends on that desire; saving faith relies on the biblical definition of hope. Biblical faith is to believe in something we can't see, and biblical hope is the sure belief that something is true or will happen. We need to be building our faith in our God so that the substance is solid.

Once Jesus decides to end this battle He will win. The interesting thing is that for now Jesus uses us to fight the battle and to move ahead His kingdom on the earth. Satan has a perceived advantage in this world because Jesus waits for us to choose Him. He wants to give us enough time to make a right choice. Maybe Satan gets a false hope from this tarrying of Jesus, maybe he just uses this time to destroy as many as he can. Either way, if we all were to choose to get fully behind Christ we all would stand as victors in this battle.

We have proven historically that we aren't, as a group, the best choice to move ahead the kingdom. But because of His love for us and His promise not to force that love upon us He allows us to muddle through with amazing results. Of course, we are not working alone. All that we do for the kingdom is lead by the Holy Spirit and He often does things differently than we would. Our enemy might use this situation to distract us in order to cast doubt on our faith. Considering the power of our enemy, using us to fight this battle is like using the local Cub Scout pack to take Iwo Jima. What are the chances that we will be victorious? We get tossed onto the beach and we are told to move ahead and take on the enemy. In this situation we don't see our back up. But even when we do things awkwardly, we have stunning success when done in a saving faith.

This could be why we, at times, are unable to fathom what is going on around us. Why is God not with me in this trial? Why isn't God hearing and responding to my prayers? We all have called out and wondered why we don't hear an answer. But do we notice when He has shown up? Sometimes when we are desperate we don't see any movement from God then "out of the blue" some wonderful thing happens and we feel back on track. It can be too easy to call this coincidence or dumb luck. In fact, that is what your enemy would like you to think. It is actually God working in His time. Keep the shield in place, do what you know how to do and wait to see what He has for you.

We must have faith in our God and in all of the armor He provides as well. The shield of faith can be used to cover the gaps in our armor but that faith also is used to fill in those gaps.

Another device of the enemy is to use our Bible against us. Be sure to dig into the Word of God as you study. There are so many times I hear misquoted or partially fleshed out teachings from the bible; or worse yet some "new revelation" coming from a teacher. Keep to the basics and use a discerning spirit when engaged in the Bible. Remember Paul's warning:

" 'But even if we, or an angel from heaven, preach any other gospel to you than what we have preached to you let them be accursed.' " (Galatians 1:8)

The fact that one large world religion bases its belief on the new revelation given to their founder by an angel from heaven is a testament to the effectiveness of Gods enemy. To claim that the Bible is the word of God but then to change the definition of Christ is an obvious deception. You can't claim to hold to the word of God and then be in violation of this basic tenant. It is fair to say that you, personally, may find a new insight for your life in a scripture that you had studied before. These revelations are based on individual circumstances but they don't offer up any new concepts.

To some these devices are painfully obvious. Those people, however, may fall for another device that they are oblivious to but is obvious to another. We must rely on God. We must trust in His word and we must allow His plan to move ahead. This requires that we have a fervent trust in his plan. This is faith.

The Cunning Dragon rightly states neither we nor anyone around us can see the object of our faith directly. When we rely on our faith many see us as foolish. By all appearances as we stand firm behind our shield all anyone can see is our arms in position but with nothing in our grasp. If we have a saving faith our position, no matter how it looks to others, is protected by the promise of Christ. So the calls of the atheists that our faith is only a myth and religion is merely a drug we use for comfort must not be allowed to hinder us. Our God is not visible because He is Spirit. Because of this the only way to accept and follow Christ is through faith.

Many have accepted Christ through faith but find it difficult to accept all He has taught about the romance, the battle and His work at the cross. If the enemy can distract us from that we become ineffective in our calling to move the kingdom of God forward while we are here.

The strength of our shield of faith comes from the fact that we must rely upon Christ for our defense and not ourselves. Its invisibility has a purpose. Not seeing Christ we have to use the full measure of our faith. This can be a conundrum for many because we often work best with solid evidence. Having to put our trust in this faith, on one hand, gives the potential for doubt. On the other hand it requires us to give the power to our God and to allow Him to be our defense.

We can't win these battles alone. We can't win these battles in small or large groups. We must do this with God at the helm. Using our faith shows that we trust in the power of the work Christ did on the cross.

From a physical point of view this is a flaw. People will see you relying on your faith and call you weak, using a crutch, relying on myth. The enemy in the spiritual realm, however, knows the power of Christ and fears it. (James 2:19) When you put your faith in Christ as your defense the enemy has to back off. Don't be fooled into thinking he won't continue to try but if you keep the strength of the shield at the ready all his fiery darts will be quenched.

There is no question that life is hard. As we struggle through this life that is what the enemy will focus on. Everything in his list of physical attacks plays to this fact. We, as physical beings, experience those struggles and can, at times, be overwhelmed by the toughness of our days. Looking at it, as Jesus wants us to, from a higher vantage point, we are to focus on His restoration of our world. The final step of that promise is in our future but we are to be working toward it now. He came to "seek and save what was lost" and to give us life "more abundantly". (Luke 19:9-11, John 10:10) This is the area the enemy wants to distract you from and that the scriptures want to lead your focus back to. Life. It was promised by Christ resurrection. We see it in His miracles. If we focus on this with our shield of Faith fully engaged the devil has no quarter.

We are dual natured. We have a physical existence and we deal with that daily. For this battle though we need to understand our spiritual nature. This is less obvious and often ignored. In order to be complete and to understand our romance and our battle we have to connect with this spiritual side.

God gives us glimpses into what we are to experience when we are finally together. We get our glimpses in the physical and we feel our longing through the spiritual. Much of the disillusionment we find ourselves dealing with in this world is a result of longing for the "more" that awaits us.

"He has put eternity in their hearts, except that no one can find out the work that God does from beginning to end."
(Ecclesiastes. 3:10)

We know there is more, much more, but because we can't see it all, or fathom it all, we feel the bulk of what is missing in this world. Don't be mistaken, however, in how you are to proceed. Though we look forward to the day when our longing is filled in heaven we are not to just sit and wait. We are to actively wait. We are called by our Lord to live as He lived. In Romans 8:1 Paul states that *"there is now no condemnation to those who are in Christ Jesus."* Jesus has already paid the price for our condemnation and The Father has already forgiven us.

The first half of the book of Romans speaks of how God does not condemn his followers. In chapter 8 he speaks of a self-condemnation. One that is not required. We have to believe we have been truly forgiven and then to get on with living our life, in front of the enemy, with the conviction that he has no power over us. The enemy will try to bring you back to this point of condemnation but Christ offers you the option to ignore the enemy. Don't open your armor to receive this poison.

Faith comes by hearing and hearing by the word of God. (Romans 10:17)

Building our faith goes beyond self. If we are to expand the Kingdom, we also need to be around those who are stronger than us and to help others develop their faith. (See Hebrews 10:24-25). If faith comes by hearing and hearing by the word of God, we must be sure all that we hear and all that we speak to others on this topic is from God's word. The enemy is an expert on counterfeiting the true meaning of the word. We have to be diligent to study it well and be faithful to pass it on un-diluted to others.

Though God can win battles with few warriors we are all called to spread the word of the gospel. When we do this we need to do it well. In Romans Paul speaks of this issue. Basically, how can one believe in Christ unless they have heard of Him from someone who is already properly in the romance? Our faith is strengthened by being immersed in the study of God and is made manifest by taking it to others. (See Romans 10:14-17)

In contrast we must guard against our human nature. This struggle is not always directly with a spiritual enemy. There are days when you are just tripping over your human nature. Not all slips are directed by the enemy but if he is paying attention they all can be used to his advantage. Don't obsess but be aware. We can defeat ourselves without much outside help. Our animal longings can bring us down as quickly as our spiritual enemy.

One of the defenses against this is to establish and build your romance with Christ. It is easier to resist temptation if your eyes remain on the romance God has planned for you. If you truly believe, truly have faith, that is what will come to pass.

"...with God all things are possible" (Matthew 19:26) Do you believe this? If not, and you are not alone if you don't, your shield needs strengthening. We have to release any covenant we have made that allows us to hang on to the idea that if God isn't doing things the way we would do them then he isn't there.

Looking into the book of Job we get some insight as to how God functions on our behalf. Over 28 chapters in Job are dedicated to the interpretation of 4 men on what they believe God expects of his people. Job and his so called friends give their opinions on what God wants and what Job must do to be restored. Job himself calls his own complaints fair because he believes what he seeks from God is reasonable.

The trouble is we can't see the end as God can. God knows why he leads us into our joys and trials but we have no way of fully comprehending His big picture. We see suffering. He sees growth and development. We feel despair and He asks us to be patient to see the outcome of our distress. Even writing this I realize how impossible it is to understand and define what God does or why He does it.

When God asks Job three verses worth of questions He is basically saying. You cannot know my ways. Job finally agrees. This is a hard thing for us. We believe that life should be fair according to our standards and that God has to act according to this "fairness". God is stating to Job that as the one who set everything in motion He is the arbiter of what is fair and just and right.

Our enemy will call upon our human nature to urge us to fight against our God holding sway over us. If times are hard we say God is not being fair or that he is not hearing us. Satan will gladly whisper agreement into our heads with those thoughts in place.

The Bible shows us that we can trust our God even when things are not going our way. It is easy to believe we can trust Him when we are content and getting what we want. We must come to understand that we will struggle, and we have to rely on God as we do so.

As I write this chapter my life has been under attack for months. We are having trouble with a failing family business and financial devastation is looming. I have, for months, believed the destruction of my finances and my household will come to fruition within a few days or weeks.

As I hang on to the truths I write about here I notice that though I am not getting the financial help I beg for, some source of income always presents itself to get me through. I trust it is God giving me just enough to get by until I am able to truly get back on my feet.

Knowing that I should have been financially spent 8 months ago I hold to my faith that Jesus is providing what I need, if not what I want, to keep me going. You can imagine how the enemy is working in my head to keep me moving down the path of believing that I have been forsaken. The whispers are that I should just give up on my God and certainly stop wasting time on this worthless book.

We are to fight this sort of attack by relying on the word of God. The book of Matthew states:

"Therefore do not worry about tomorrow, for tomorrow will worry about its own things. Sufficient for the day is its own trouble." (Matthew 6:34)

And the book of Luke states

And which of you by worrying can add one cubit to his stature?" If you then are not able to do the least, why are you anxious for the rest?" (Luke 12:25-26)

It may be hard during times of struggle to rest in those words but if Jesus didn't mean it He wouldn't have said it. I have chosen to believe it and Jesus invites you to do the same.

When our enemy speaks, he speaks a lie.

"When he lies, he speaks his native tongue" (John 8:44).

When I feel discouraged by doing work to teach others, or myself, the things of God, I now assume it is because of the whispers of the enemy. The enemy uses the Bible against us, but he uses it out of context or with deception. In the latter part of John 8:44 When Jesus calls Satan the father of lies we do well to heed this warning.

The Cunning Dragon relates the story of the 7 sons of Sceva to his audience, but he only reveals the part he wants to use to make a point to his troops. He stops when the story stops making him look good. The continuation of that story shows how God's purpose is fulfilled and the name of Jesus is magnified. When learning either from self study or from another's commentary be sure to follow up the work for verification.

When we first accept Christ into our hearts we are sure we want this relationship. At this stage it can be more of an infatuation. As we grow, as in any long-term relationship, some of the emotional response dissipates and we are left to feel that we lost something. When seeking this romance keep in mind that Love is not an emotion, it is knowledge. I know I love my wife even when we aren't getting along, or when we are just coasting. We still have our wonderful times of emotional connection but we don't stop loving each other when those times wane. The same is true with your romance with Christ. Don't be fooled by the endorphin rush when things are heady versus the intellectual knowledge that the love exists outside of that emotion.

The chief goal of the enemy is to cause us to fail in this love but without showing his face. He uses to his advantage the fact that he is in the spirit as well. We can no easier point to the enemy as we can to God. Knowledge of both requires our faith.

His objective is to remain hidden, camouflaged, so all that goes wrong can be blamed on you, the fickle circumstances of life or on God himself. Though our troubles can be caused or allowed by these three things, everything we do to repel the enemy will hinder the amount and severity of a true spiritual attack. Using the full armor of God to protect ourselves against all comers will guarantee the desired outcome in proper time.

Our goal, then, should be to prevent openings in our defenses. The thing that grows in our life is the thing that we feed.

*"Do not be deceived, God is not mocked;
for whatever a man sows, that he will also reap.
For he who sows to his flesh will of the flesh reap corruption,
but he who sows to the spirit will of the spirit reap everlasting life."*
(Galatians 6:7-8)

The deception spoken of in the first line of this verse may either come from the enemy or us but it will never come from God. By His very nature God is incapable of deception.

*"Every good and perfect gift is from above,
and comes down from the Father of Lights,
with whom there is no variation or shadow of turning."*
(James 1:17)

Through all the devices available to the Cunning Dragon he will do all he can to deceive us into falling from our desire to please God.

2 Peter 2:1-4 speaks of how false teachers will deceive many who will follow them. The last line of these verses is *"…and their destruction does not slumber."* Because of this we are always a target. Again, do not be obsessive in this endeavor but be vigilant.

The more time we stay focused on the things of this world the more fruit we will produce from the flesh. This makes us an easier target. It seems to be much harder to stay focused on the things of the Spirit but that is because this world cries out against it and the enemy does whatever he can to direct you away from the spiritual truth.

Don't allow yourself to be disillusioned by the constant effort by our enemy to wear you down. If that thought should overtake you lean into the words of Christ and trust his promise. It is true that His burden is light but we have to develop an understanding of what is required of us. The further we get into that understanding the lighter the burden. Partially because the more we rely on Christ the less opportunities the enemy has to penetrate a chink in our armor.

Keep returning to the word and the study of God. Allow yourself to be enveloped by the romance. An error we make is putting our human expectations into the eternal timeframe of God. I am often let down by the expectations I place on my relationship with God because I interject expectations never offered by Him. God said he will never leave us or forsake us. (Deut. 31:6) But when we put a time frame or defined outcome to our requests we let ourselves down. The enemy would like us to blame God for these emotions. Guard against that.

The Battle, the Love, and the Reward.

A quick look at the bible shows it to be at least three things: Descriptions of the battle in which we are engaged both in the spiritual and physical worlds, a story of the love offered to us by God, and the fulfillment of the prophecy of the coming of Christ to save us and to lead us in the victory in that battle with it's ultimate reward.

The Battle

A ploy of the enemy is to whisper that you are not to fight; that there is, in fact, nothing to fight for or against. But Jesus calls us to battle the powers and principalities of this world.

In the Book of Revelation the Lord comes with a sword in his hand and in Ephesians He hands us ours,

"The sword of the spirit, which is the word of God." (Ephesians 6:17)

The word of God is a complex and effective tool. We do well to study it and use it properly, as God intended it, for our defense. It has many other purposes as well, but the proper use of the word will strengthen our defenses. As an example of that Jesus used it exclusively to repel Satan during his temptation in the wilderness. And He knew it well enough that Satan could not use a distortion of it against Him. It will take time for us to get there but our time is invested well in this pursuit.

Any sword, including The Word of God, is both a defensive and an offensive weapon. The rest of the armor is decisively for our defense, but we rely on the word of God to both build up our armor and to move ahead when engaged in battle.

The description of the armor shows that God calls us, into a battle. We are created in His image and a definitive part of that image is one of a warrior. If we fall back to the images we have seen on our Sunday school walls we will see a gentle loving man who cradles sheep and plays kindly with children. This is certainly one of the aspects of Christ. But another aspect of our God, and the one we need to fully understand for this part of our struggle, is how He presents Himself when an enemy is attacking His sheep or children.

"The Lord is a warrior; the Lord is His name." (Exodus 15:3, NIV).

Many of us have been led to see Jesus as "meek and mild", as a kind, gentle and harmless man. That is not the God presented in the Bible. Christ, Himself, states

"' And from the days of John the Baptist until now the kingdom of Heaven suffers violence and the violent take it by force.' " (Matthew 11:12)

There are a few views on what this passage indicates. One leads the follower of Christ to prepare for a violent struggle to retake the Kingdom another indicates that violence will be used in an attempt to keep that kingdom at bay. Either way, for a believer in Christ, it is a call to battle. We must enter in and defend our position and push back the enemy. We aren't called to just hold our ground we are called to advance God's Kingdom here on earth.

" '…and on this rock I will build my church, and the gates of Hades shall not prevail against it. And I will give you the keys of the kingdom of heaven, and whatever you bind on earth will be bound in heaven,
and whatever you loose on earth will be loosed in heaven.' "
(Matthew 16:18-19)

There is controversy by theologians over what is referenced by the rock that the church is built upon. You can choose Peter, whose name was changed by Jesus to the "Little Rock" or Peter's profession that Jesus was not a profit but the Messiah, or on Christ Himself who Peter later reminds us is the cornerstone of the foundation of our faith (1Peter 2:4-6). In the end all of these options can be distilled down to this:

If we profess Christ as our Lord and Savior, as Peter did, we are in possession of the power and authority of Christ.

This point brings up a warning. Outside of the essentials required for our faith there are many things we, as Christians, can debate. Which of the three options above did Christ want us to understand? If we loose site of the goal and fight among ourselves we are weakening our position. This is a tactic mentioned by the Cunning Dragon. Iron sharpening iron is a good biblical principal but don't let the sharpening turn into a sword fight that damages and dulls your blades. Approach all these debates in love. If it starts to turn to a battle that doesn't move the Kingdom of God forward, back down. We will know all of the answers in due time. Have fun in the discussions and wait until you can ask Jesus for the final answer.

" '... If God is for us, who can be against us?' " (Romans 8:31)

In this passage Paul speaks of the power that backs us and the confidence we have in that protection. He also speaks to the spiritual battle and our assurance there.

" Who shall separate us from the love of Christ? Shall tribulation, or distress, or persecution, or famine, or nakedness, or peril, or sword?
As it is written: "For your sake we are killed all day long;
We are accounted as sheep for the slaughter."
Yet in all these things we are more than conquerors through Him who loved us.
For I am persuaded that neither death nor life, nor angels nor principalities nor powers, not things present nor things to come, nor height nor depth, nor any other created thing, shall be able to separate us from the love of God which is in Christ Jesus our Lord' "(Romans 8:35-39)

Paul uses the same reference to Satan and his followers here as he does in Ephesians. Our major fight is against the powers and principalities of darkness. Though we struggle with our flesh and the desires of this world we must not let them become the tools that the demons use to effect our fall. Be aware of your enemy but do not be obsessed. Your focus should always be on Christ.

In the book of Romans Paul advises us of what to rely on and what to avoid.

" But if the Spirit of Him who raised Jesus from the dead dwells in you,
He who raised Christ from the dead will also give life to your mortal bodies through His Spirit who dwells in you.

Therefore, brethren, we are debtors—not to the flesh, to live according the flesh.
For if you live according to the flesh you will die; but if by the Spirit you put to death the deeds of the body, you will live.
For as many as are lead by the Spirit of God, these are the sons of God.' " (Romans 8:11-14)

We are indwelt with the same Spirit that raised Jesus from the dead. That is a most powerful tool. The only weakness we have is in how we use our freedom. We must choose. God will not force his love on us. In order to make headway in this battle you must choose Christ daily. If God gives us the grace to renew His mercy daily (Lamentations 3:22-24) we need to offer ourselves back to Him for renewal daily as well. (1cor 4:16)

We must also make a deliberate attempt to return to Him after every slip. Paul wrote to the Galatians about the law being fulfilled in the action of love. In that context he states,

" *'I say then: walk in the Spirit, and you shall not fulfill the lust of the flesh. For the flesh lusts against the Spirit, and the Spirit against the flesh; and these are contrary to one another, so that you do not do the things you wish' ." (Gal 5:16-17)*

Even someone with Paul's background struggled with the flesh; and he recognizes the fact that we all will struggle. The key is to renew yourself daily in

Christ to overcome your weakness. We win this battle not through our strength but in the strength of the Holy Spirit.

"...He who is in you is greater than he who is in the world." *(1John 4:4)*

The enemy will do and say anything he can to shift you from this truth. He wants you to fear and falter. He will use the trials and tribulations of this world to discourage you. He wants you to give in to the ease of the life he offers and reject the call to the romance Christ offers. When things don't go as you plan he will use those down times to lure you from God; to make you believe that you have been mistaken in your quest; to cause you to give up and just give in to your lusts and frailties.

If you wait until you are beat up to seek help you may be easily drawn away. Spend time every day in the romance. Seek God even when you don't feel the need. Take time to sit at His feet and just listen. Go to Him when you don't need anything in particular and see where He might lead you. Just take the time to unplug and let his peace and calm run over you. Then, when the enemy has you up against the ropes, you will not have any guilt when you ask for help from God.

Satan is a master at luring us away from this relationship with other offers and encouragements. Then, when we are beat up and need help he will cry out. "How can you ask for help now after ignoring your God for so long? He won't listen to you. He has forgotten you." If we take the time to renew our love daily, these tricks will have little power.

The key to overcoming this enemy is to move closer to God. There are many examples in the Bible of God's people believing He doesn't listen to them anymore and because of this belief they move further away. (See Ezekiel Chapter 8) But without exception, as His people move away, God gives them a chance to return to Him. He is patient and long-suffering. He promises justice but avoids it to the end for our sakes. Do not let your enemy lead you to believe otherwise. When you are immersed in this romance and investing your time learning of your beloved you will know that in times of trouble He is still there. Trust the armor, stay close to God and he will stay close to you.

Even though we are fully equipped by God to win that does not allow us to be passive. This is an active pursuit. We must move ahead the Kingdom of God by the direction of the Spirit. In Revelation Christ returns as a warrior on a horse fully prepared for battle. (Rev 19:11-16) We are to continue this battle until then.

THE LOVE

This love affair is decidedly one sided. Though we are to be engaged we fall away easily. When God speaks through the words and life of the prophet Hosea the example He gives is apropos to us as Christians just as it was to the people of Israel.

As an example of how He views His condition of His romance with us he has Hosea take a prostitute as his wife. The marriage of Hosea to Gomer, the harlot, is destined for hardship. Though she is Hosea's wife she desires to return to her illicit life. And she does this over and over again leaving Hosea alone.

Hosea, though, is called by God to return to his wife.

"Go again, love a woman who is loved by a lover and is committing adultery, just like the love of the lord for the children of Israel, who took to other gods and love the raisin cakes of the pagans." (Hosea 3:1)

Reading the books of the prophets of the Old Testament shows our weakness and how we fall to our human nature. The example of the marriage of Hosea and Gomer shows an uncommon graciousness. Most, put in that position, would rightfully walk away from the relationship. It could certainly no longer be called a romance. That is unless the faithful lover could truly overlook the transgression and erase the feelings we would expect them to have.

This is what Christ promises to do for us. As incomprehensible as it might appear to us, even when we cheat on God, God is able and willing to forgive and forget.

Stop for a moment and consider this. No matter the violation, no matter the intent, if anyone is truly repentant God graciously and completely takes them back. And in the moment after forgiveness He returns to the joy of the romance as though nothing improper has ever occurred. I might not be able to do that, you might not be able to do that but He does. This is the power of the romance and why it seems incomplete to call it just a relationship.

The proof of the strength of this romance is the compilation, as told by the Prophets, of the continual and repeated infraction of God's people against it. Through it all God retains a remnant of his people to assure his promises are fulfilled. When we consider this offering from God, we have to take seriously the words of Paul of Christ's grace. He speaks of the unparalleled grace offered to us by Christ even in our sin. Then he asks:

" What shall we say then?
Shall we continue in sin that grace may abound?
Certainly not!' " (Romans 6:1-2)

But how can you not fall into this romance knowing what you have done to tarnish it and yet knowing God will polish that tarnish away. We will likely still have to endure the consequences of our actions but even in that chastened state we are welcomed back.

It may be easier, by nature, for women to understand the romance of Christ and for men to understand the battle for his kingdom. Both are essential elements for God's plan but we tend to focus ourselves differently. Focus on what you feel your heart to be called to but be a student of both of these aspects of the kingdom.

In his book "Wild at Heart", John Eldredge states that there are three things that a man desires: "A battle to fight, an adventure to live and a beauty to rescue". We live these things everyday in our physical realm. Sometimes we do them well as in respectful competition, a climbing adventure and wooing our wives. Sometime we are caught up in the distortions from this world such as engaging in a bar fight, succumbing to road rage or turning to pornography. They are part of our nature here and we must look to how they can be effectively used in the spirit and how not to succumb to their abuse.

All three are essential for us to advance God's Kingdom. The battle to fight is for the protection and expansion of God's Kingdom, the beauty to rescue is our relationship with Jesus, (What could be more beautiful than the promised marriage of us, the church, to Christ?) and the adventure to live is ongoing in both of those processes. Our enemy wants to take all three, and more, from us.

The three corresponding desires for women as described by John and Stacy Eldredge in their book

"Captivating" are: to be "swept up into adventure, to play an irreplaceable role in a great romance and to be the beauty of the story". Men and women were created to display different aspects of God's nature but you can see how these basic characteristics overlap.

Women too seek adventure and are effective warriors. They too want to be engulfed in this pure romance and, because God made them the crowning glory of creation, they rightly crave to be recognized as a beauty in Christ's story.

Both men and women, in order to be effective for God, need to shift their focus on these elements from the corruption of this world to the perfection of God's spiritual plan. Remember that we are saved unto salvation. No matter how hard we try perfection will not be achieved until the return of Christ. This is a fact that the enemy will use to dissuade you from continuing on this path. Our calling is to do what we can, with what God has given us, to keep pressing ahead.

Because Christ was a man it may be hard for men to embrace this romance by that term. We would be better equipped to understand it if Christ came as a woman. The biggest problem with that would have been many more would have followed her but nearly all of them would have followed for the wrong reasons. To fully embrace this romance, we have to pull ourselves out of the gender role issues and out of the desire for Eros in a romance. This is about true and complete fulfillment not about the temporary satisfaction of erotic love. Better to think of all that you desire in the love from your father and the respect and love from a male friend who you also respect and love. Christ gives an array of examples of how he longs for His people. All speak of perfect love. None, with the exception of the "Song of Solomon", even hint at the erotic. When considering your connection to Jesus as something more than just a relationship. Reflect on the love offered to us by Christ through the example of the Prodigal Son and His call to Jerusalem.

When the Prodigal Son left home with his inheritance, squandered it all and found himself in dire straights, He humbly went home to work as a servant for his father. When his father saw that he was coming home his love was shown by his reaction.

"...and when he was still a great way off, his father saw him and had compassion, and ran and fell on his neck and kissed him." (Luke 15:20)

As the story continues, the father has his servants dress his son in a robe, put sandals on his feet and place the family ring upon his hand. Then he calls for a feast to celebrate. All that is required for full forgiveness and restoration is that the son willingly returns.

In His call to Jerusalem, Jesus talks to the leaders of His people citing their transgressions.

" 'How often I wanted to gather your children together, as a hen gathers her chicks under her wings, but you were not willing.' "
(Matthew 23:37)

He desires the romance, but He will not force us. That, in itself speaks of a higher love. The Biblical accounts of this love are numerous and all point to the depth of love offered and desired from Jesus.

The Reward

As we wander around on this fallen earth it is easy to lose heart. We find that there is little that truly fulfills us. We seek something and we follow after it and when we achieve it, it feels empty.

Solomon uses a whole book of the Bible to describe this emptiness. He called it vanity or vapor. He who had everything this world could give him was empty inside. Our experience and his words define the truth of this ailment.

"Meaningless! Meaningless!"
Says the teacher.
Utterly meaningless!
Everything is meaningless."
(Ecclesiastes 1:2)

These words from Solomon ring true to most of us. They are the cry of the man who seeks to find fulfillment in this world.

" 'All things are wearisome,
more than one can say.
The eye never has enough of seeing,
nor the ear its fill of hearing.' "
(Ecclesiastes 1:8-9)

What is it that we long for and why is it that no man has ever found it?

" 'I have seen the burden God has laid on men.
He has made everything beautiful in its time.
He has also set eternity in the hearts of men; yet they cannot fathom what God has done from beginning to end.' "
(Ecclesiastes 3:10-11)

It is that "eternity in the hearts of men" that unsettles us. We were created to experience the joy of a perfected life in communion with God. This is lost in practice but still dwells in our hearts. *The enemy knows this*. It is the key to his attack. He knows our desire for that complete satisfaction that we were designed for and he uses that desire to draw us away. He offers us a counterfeit, at a price, to everything God offers to us freely. He reminds us how empty this life can be and he counts on that fact to weaken our resolve.

So, you are not alone in this disillusionment. This world is nothing compared to how it was designed to be and how it will be once it is restored. We all falter because the longing we have for that restored world is still in our hearts even as we struggle to make some semblance of it in this corrupted existence.

A desire has been placed within us to seek that perfected state. We innately know it is out there and we long for it. When we rely on this world to fulfill it we are disappointed. If we wait for it to find us we will miss our opportunity to be used by God to help advance His kingdom. We fall into the enemy's plan when we focus only on the feeling we get from the lack of fulfillment. We must work through the valleys but focus on the things that reveal God to us in this world.

We need to find the hints, the glimpses, of the fulfilled promise in our lives and understand that the whole picture will not be visible to any of us here. This is not a cause for depression or despair. Compare it to the coming of your highly awaited vacation to the location of your dreams. You have to fill in the blanks here because your ideal vacation may differ from what is presented, but follow along.

You plan and save and make reservations for your first trip to an island in the Bahamas. As you confirm your travel plans you can picture the deserted sand beach and the sounds of the waves sweeping up to the shore. You mentally reach out to feel the comfortable moist heat of the sun, the scent of the salt air and the perfume of the lush plants beyond the beach. It is heavenly!

But for now, you sit at your desk at work after commuting for 45 minutes through the ice and snow. You are still affected by the cold experienced during your walk from the car to the office. There is a familiar scent to your office, but it doesn't offer the promise of relaxation only the reminder of the duties of the day. As you prepare for your day your computer screen flashes on and the picture of your beach comes to life. You can imagine the landscape and almost smell the salt air. That feeling is the one you want to experience always. Then you are brought back to your responsibilities at the office.

Heaven, for us, is that place where we are going, haven't yet really experienced but dream of regularly. If you don't dream of it you must start. It is the prize that makes this life and the spiritual battle worthwhile. (I assume the reader is already a true follower of Christ and is already destined to this outcome. If you are not, that is your next step.)

Not losing heart will require diligence. We want so much more; we have been promised so much more but all we see is what surrounds us on the general landscape. We are promised the Bahamas, but we dwell in our office.

To find your strength look for these snippets of heaven. Think of Heaven as you would the vacation scenario above. But more than that use the hints God gives to experience the passing moments of that joy. We all have those triggers. The scent of lilac, the exquisite flavor of a fresh ripe raspberry or the place in our mind we go to when we hear that piece of music or the warble of our favorite songbird. Whenever these snippets arise, experience that moment. Bask in it. Be immersed. When I see a hawk or a falling star I consider it a love note from God. These things bring me joy and I know joy is God's promise to me. When they present themselves I make a conscious effort to be overtaken by them. No matter what else is going on I indulge myself and acknowledge my Lord in that moment.

This is where I draw my strength. This is where I push aside the misdirection of the evil one and refocus my intention. I have been assured of heaven (2 Corinthians 5:8) and I am ready to go but as long as I am needed here I will take comfort in the snippets expressed to me by God. (See Philippians 1:21-24) It excites me to know that when the time comes to be present with Christ every moment will be filled with the joy that is only temporary here.

The question, "Won't you get bored being in heaven ***forever!***?" comes from those who imagine the myth that heaven is comprised of sitting on a cloud and playing a harp. First, we won't experience time as we do now. In fact, we may not experience time at all. When we accept each moment as it is passed on to us and completely engage in the offering, we will not even know how much time is spent in that moment or with that experience. And because the time will be spent in complete joy there will be nothing going on that we will want to end. Time will not matter.

By contrast this life is hard, this life is a burden, and this life will drain joy from you if you don't act deliberately. Take the small moments offered to you, those snippets of heaven, and use them to recharge.

The key to overcoming the despair expressed by Solomon in Ecclesiastes is to go to the end and see where he leads us. It is all summed up in one sentence.

"Fear God and keep his commandments, for this is the whole duty of man."
(Ecclesiastes 12:13)

If your relationship with Jesus is a romance, then on this path you will define "duty" as a joyful obligation. When you can do this, you will find victory in this battle. Choosing God is an active pursuit. Choosing Satan is a default position, which requires only a passive stance.

" Be sober, be vigilant; because your adversary the devil walks about like a roaring lion, seeking whom he may devour. Resist

him steadfast in the faith, knowing the same sufferings are experienced by your brotherhood in the world.' "
(1Peter 5-8)

While following the words of Peter it is critical to take C.S. Lewis' words from *The Screwtape Letters* to heart. In the preface he states: "There are two equal and opposite errors into which our race can fall about the devils. One is to disbelieve in their existence. The other is to believe, and to feel an excessive and unhealthy interest in them. They themselves are equally pleased by both errors and hail a materialist or a magician with the same delight."

How do we stay aware of the devils but not become obsessed? How do we discern if the mild depression that overcomes us on a particular morning is an attack from Satan or too much sugar in last night's bedtime snack? Don't spend as much time on the cause as you do focusing on Christ and a Biblical solution. Don't look for a demon behind every shrub. But don't assume that they won't do their best to affect you either. The way to handle your Christian life is to rely on biblical direction and proper action. Sometimes we have to take a stand against evil by using the authority of Christ given to us by his work on the cross. Sometimes we just need to rest and refocus our lives to be able to deal simply with what life has for us today.

The winning of both these battles rely on leaning into Christ. He is the solution, He is our rest, and He is our Sabbath. Whether your trials are spirit caused or from the physical world use the tenets of His teaching to build strength and overcome your distress. Sometimes it will be easy other times not. Never overly focus on the cause but on the solution.

"A wise man will hear and increase learning
and a man of understanding will obtain wise counsel"
(Proverbs 1:5)

John 1:1 defines Christ personally as the Word of God, and the Bible in its entirety is the written word of God. The word of God, then, is our wise counsel. Seek your counsel from the Bible and from mature believers.

The Call

Find strength when you are being attacked. This suggests you are a worthy target. You must be doing something effectively to draw the attention of your enemy. Righteously hold your head high in this situation. Draw strength from this and don't be drained. We are always a potential point of attack when we hinder anything coming against God's Kingdom. When our work becomes powerful and obvious we are serving our King well! When this happens, instead of curling up, call to Christ and draw from His strength.

What makes this battle worth entering is the romance and the reward. If you truly love God, you will want to work on His behalf. If you are aware of the rewards promised us, you will want to be certain that you influence everyone in your circle to move in the direction that allows them that reward as well. A real battle is ongoing. It is easy to ignore it and a danger to take this information casually.

In a scene from the movie "Braveheart" our situation is represented. Several Scotsmen lined up on the battlefield see the enemy across the field and decide it would be better if they left so that they might live. In the story William Wallace, who is leading the attack against the English says:

"Ay, fight and you may die, run and you'll live. At least a while. And dying in your beds many years from now, would you be willing to trade all the days from this day to that for one chance, just one chance to come back here and tell our enemies that they may take our lives… but they'll never take our freedom."

We must make the same considerations. Certainly if you have given your life to Christ you are saved. You will reach heaven. You will be forever with God. You could leave the field and not have the additional struggles that come with the fight. But wouldn't it be better, when you are in the presence of Christ, to be able to look with Him upon the time you spent in His service fighting for the advancement of His kingdom in your world? Wouldn't it be better to look around at the people who are there because you allowed yourself to be used by God instead of wondering who is not there because you went home satisfied that your personal salvation was enough?

Now is the time to put on your protective gear, your armor, and to be willing to be led by your Lord wherever He wants to use you.

"Be sober, be vigilant; because your adversary the devil walks about like a roaring lion, seeking whom he may devour. Resist him steadfast in the faith."
1 Peter 5:8

This is our call to arms. Resist him! But don't think first of the battle, think first of the rewards. Think first of what is worth fighting for.

Then resist him.

About the Author
Randal Kinkade is founder and director of The Willow River Wilderness School where he teaches private and corporate classes based on primitive technology.

He lives in Tucson, Arizona.

He is devoted to helping people learn about the outdoors and to reach their true Christian objectives.

For more information go to the website:
www.willowriverwilderness.com